Building Shared Responsibility for Student Learning

Anne Conzemius and Jan O'Neill

Association for Supervision
and Curriculum Development

Alexandria, Virginia USA

Association for Supervision and Curriculum Development
1703 N. Beauregard St. • Alexandria, VA 22311-1714 USA
Telephone: 1-800-933-2723 or 703-578-9600 • Fax: 703-575-5400
Web site: http://www.ascd.org • E-mail: member@ascd.org

Printed in the United States of America.

December 2001 member book (p). ASCD Premium, Comprehensive, and Regular members
periodically receive ASCD books as part of their membership benefits. No. FY02-03.

Paperback ISBN: 0-87120-597-1 • ASCD product #101039 • List Price: $23.95
($19.95 ASCD member price, direct from ASCD only)
e-books ($23.95): netLibrary ISBN 0-87120-982-9 • ebrary ISBN 0-87120-983-7

Library of Congress Cataloging-in-Publication Data
Conzemius, Anne, 1953–
    Building shared responsibility for student learning / Anne Conzemius
and Jan O'Neill.
         p. cm.
Includes bibliographical references and index.
    ISBN 0-87120-597-1 (alk. paper)
    1. School improvement programs. 2. School environment. 3. Group work in education.
I. O'Neill, Jan, 1955– II. Title.
    LB2822.8 .C66 2001
    371.2'07—dc21
                                                                        2001006467

06 05 04   10 9 8 7 6 5 4 3 2

For Luke

Building Shared Responsibility for Student Learning

Acknowledgments

Some of our colleagues warned us that the process of writing a book together would range anywhere from "challenging" to "difficult" to downright *painful*. Fortunately, this proved not to be the case. Writing this book has offered us the opportunity to reflect on our collective 40+ years of work in both education and the quality movement. It's given us the chance to think carefully about how to present methods and tools that are proving useful in the schools where we've worked. Most importantly, in writing this book, we have been able to honor the work of clients and colleagues who are deeply committed to building shared responsibility for student learning.

Every finished work bears the invisible stamp of the teachers who stood to its side and influenced its outcome through their words, their actions, their *being*. Many teachers stand to the side of the work we present here. Throughout the years and at key points, they have stirred our minds, our hearts, and our souls. Dr. W. Edwards Deming has had a profound impact on how we think about the nature of quality, work, management, and systems. His early manuscript for *Out of the Crisis* is a revered treasure on our bookshelf. The late statistician Dr. William G. Hunter believed in each individual's ability to bring joy and inspiration to the workplace. His words, "Why not try it and see what happens?" still ring in our ears. Through their contributions to the quality movement, Dr. Brian L. Joiner and Peter Scholtes have demonstrated the power of data and of teams when they unite around a shared purpose. It was a pleasure working with and learning from them both.

We credit Patrick Dolan, a mentor and friend, with planting the seeds of shared responsibility in education. Through his heartfelt, humorous, and provocative stories and flipchart art, he has inspired thousands of educators, parents, and community members to work together for systemic change focused on student learning. Rick DuFour's work in creating Professional Learning Communities has proven that change theories built on a foundation of vision, mission, values, and goals really do work in practice.

More recently, we have had the good fortune to get to know and learn from Linda Lambert and Parker Palmer, two teachers in whose presence one always feels more confident and sure. Their support, encouragement, and thoughtful questions always invite us to feel a little bit deeper and think a little bit wider. We are grateful to have had the opportunity to learn from—and with—such exceptional learners and teachers.

In addition, we wish to acknowledge the many contributions our clients and colleagues have made to this work. Their ability to translate theory into action—to put continuous improvement tools, methods, and philosophy into practice—enriches us all. Their students, teachers, and families are indeed fortunate to have them in their lives.

We would also like to thank Anne Meek, our ASCD editor, for her encouragement, helpful "midwifery," and her confidence in us. Her insights and experience were just what our book needed. Sue Reynard, our QLD editor, always contributes a steadying hand, a clear and honest eye, and a wonderful sense of balance to the work we do; as with all our projects, we couldn't have done this one without her guidance. And our thanks, as always, to Michelle Larson, our assistant at QLD. Organization, people skills, a flair for graphics, and great good humor are just a few of her many talents.

Finally, a special thanks to our family and friends, in particular Bill and Hank, for putting up with us over these past several months. You have always supported, encouraged, and believed in us, no matter what. For this, and many things, we are grateful.

ANNE CONZEMIUS and JAN O'NEILL
Quality Leadership by Design, LLC
Madison, Wisconsin
July 2001

Foreword

By Linda Lambert

Today's educators live in a time of "choosing urgency." We choose urgency over reason and knowledge; we choose urgency over what we know is best for children. These choices are often served up pre-packaged, on one-size-fits-all plates. Curriculum is narrowed, especially for poor, urban children. Test content becomes the curriculum. Decontextualized memorization replaces thoughtful instruction. Short-term jumps in standardized test scores mask the lack of true learning, until two years down the road, when scores level out and then begin to decline.

Why make such choices? Political pressure on state legislatures? The tenure of school boards and superintendents? A deep lack of understanding of what constitutes learning accountability? A last-ditch fight for the survival of public schooling? Perhaps all of the above.

Educators are being held "accountable," but we are not holding ourselves "responsible." Accountability conjures up an "outside in" process, and responsibility is more likely an "inside out" process. Like knowledge, when responsibility is generated from within, from the learner and the community, it is collective and it attends to *real* learning and *real* evidence rather than fleeting numbers.

In this book, Anne Conzemius and Jan O'Neill blaze a path to educational responsibility—to *shared* responsibility for student learning. Shared responsibility, the authors tell us, occurs when school staffs identify what they mean by "success" and understand that to achieve success is to truly make a difference in children's lives. Staff members learn through change, thereby committing themselves to the outcomes. And this learning takes place as the result of common *focus, collaboration,* and *reflection*; leadership becomes a matter of shared responsibility because leadership is purposeful learning together in community.

Fortunately for educators, Conzemius and O'Neill do more than tell us about the journey toward shared responsibility for student learning: In this remarkable little book, they show us how it is done, and thus provide a guiding beacon of sanity through the dark sea of turbulent accountability schemes. Their conceptual framework for building shared responsibility creates a dynamic complexity among three critical elements: focus, collaboration, and reflection. The authors use stories, examples, tools, and strategies to help us understand the work at a deep level and to encourage us to leverage the examples and tools into substantive knowledge.

Linda Lambert is a Professor and Director of the Center for Educational Leadership at California State University, Haywood (CSUH).

Many educators today report feeling overwhelmed. Our world is fragmented by too many demands and initiatives and little clarity about what's important. We are being asked to do it all. *Focus* is the way of thinking that brings core values, mission, and vision to life and keeps them as the centerpiece of our professional lives. Focus helps us brush away the less meaningful in pursuit of the meaningful, the irrelevant in pursuit of the most relevant.

The authors describe *reflection* as "the use of data for improvement," and they tell us it can and should become a habit of mind. What does this really mean? When we habitually reflect, both personally and in collaboration with others, we internalize the essential questions of professional practice. Reflection enables us to test our assumptions and create distance from the urgent in order to discover the important. Such habits require the democratization of data—it must be discovered, brought to the open, and shared for all to consider.

Focus and reflection are upheld by *collaboration*. "Without collaboration," the authors insist, "our knowledge goes unleveraged, our data unused." Further, they point out that collaboration is skillful work and is situated in interdependent relationships. "It is about creating an environment—through structures, systems, processes, and policies—where everyone contributes skills, knowledge, and experience to continuously improve student learning." The puzzled observer is quick to realize that this kind of work does not come naturally to educators. Prepared to teach children, we have not found it easy to translate our good instructional skills into leadership skills with adults. Once again, the authors describe the work to be done, provide rich examples, and sketch the evolution of collaborative groups.

They also address "SMART goals," those improvement-minded outcomes we focus on, reflect in, and collaborate about. SMART goals are sensible, specific, doable, and based on data and best professional judgment. Success with SMART goals leads to teacher efficacy and student learning. What's more, these goals stimulate our appetite for success—a yearning best satisfied by experience with success itself.

There is a robust movement underway to separate leadership from leader—to recast leadership as a broad cultural concept distinguished from role, position, and the discrete set of skills of an individual. This view of leadership allows those who have abdicated natural leadership roles to see themselves and their values reflected in a process that encompasses purpose, learning, and responsibility. The most frequently asked question I hear about leadership capacity is this: "We know what our schools look like now, and we know how we want them to look, but how do we get there?" Conzemius and O'Neill show us a promising path.

No tribute is more honoring than to have talented authors take your work to a new level of complexity and application. The authors have accomplished that deed by showing persuasively that enhanced leadership capacity is the outcome of the shared responsibility framework. The educators whose voices we hear in this book have accepted responsibility for student learning, and in doing so, they have discovered that they are leaders.

Building Shared Responsibility for Student Learning is broad and it is deep. It begins with a rich conceptual framework, then expands to tell the stories and share the examples of real schools as they do the work of building shared responsibility. Throughout, the authors present graphic tools, artifacts, assessments, and exercises that enable us to walk away with a profound and comprehensive understanding of what it means to build shared responsibility. Through an artful weaving of significant research, the felt voices of educators, and practical examples and tools, Anne Conzemius and Jan O'Neill have brought together in a new way the best of what is known today.

Wisdom in the field of education is a commodity in great demand and short supply. I am optimistic that when educators read this wise book, fewer districts will choose the current road of urgency, and more will realize that we have within ourselves the power to find the Holy Grail all educators and communities seek: deep learning for all children within a sensible time frame.

Introduction

If you walk into Savanna Oaks Elementary School and ask the question, "Who here is responsible for student learning?" you will get one reply, in myriad voices.

"I am," the teachers will state.

"I am," the secretary will respond.

"I am," the students will tell you.

"I am," the parents will say.

"I am," the principal will affirm.

Who is responsible for student learning at Savanna Oaks?

Answer: Everyone.

You can sense and see shared responsibility in everything that happens at Savanna Oaks. Teachers work collaboratively to evaluate and improve their instructional strategies. Some teachers manage their own programs, handling everything from staffing to budgets to assessing their own effectiveness; from time to time, the principal checks in to make sure these teachers have what they need to be successful. With the help of teachers and parents, Savanna Oaks students are setting individual learning goals and monitoring their own progress toward these goals. Parents from all parts of the school community are active in the school's governance and partner with the administration and teachers to set school policy.

Shared responsibility at Savanna Oaks is a feeling that "what I do makes a difference in how well students learn." That feeling exists because everyone has both the knowledge they need to make informed decisions about how best to promote learning and the skills and opportunity to translate their ideas into effective action. It is *shared* responsibility because these individuals see themselves as part of a larger system, where all the pieces work together toward a common goal.

Located in Verona, Wisconsin, within a district serving a community with some of the wealthiest and some of the poorest children in the county, Savanna Oaks has more children receiving free and reduced lunch than any other school in the district. It also has the highest mobility rate and the widest discrepancy between high and low socio-economic status (SES). Its test scores, however, are consistently at—and in some cases, even above—district and state averages.

The Challenge of Emulating Success

What can educators learn from the example of successful schools like Savanna Oaks? Recently, a group of administrators contacted our organization, Quality Leadership by Design (QLD), seeking the answer to a very similar question. They wanted to visit some of the successful schools we work with to learn which programs or organizational designs these schools had implemented.

Although we encouraged the administrators to visit several schools (Savanna Oaks included), we also cautioned them that what they would see would not be "programs" or specific school designs per se, but rather best organizational and instructional practices in action. Despite our words of warning, the administrators returned from their site visits frustrated. "These schools aren't using anything in particular!" they reported. "They've incorporated lots of bits and pieces and have come up with their own approaches."

And therein lies the biggest challenge facing schools and school districts interested in developing shared responsibility for student learning: It's not a program. It's not a curriculum. Shared responsibility incorporates a set of principles and techniques that give members of the school community the authority and responsibility to create what is needed, based on the data and culture of their particular school and school district. We believe it is this ability to *learn, adopt, modify, and innovate* that makes schools like Savanna Oaks successful.

The quest to find instant answers and capture "the secrets of school success" via programs and designs lies at the root of the problem with "benchmarking" as it is implemented by many educators. We're all familiar with the drill: Get the most recent "best" program, arrange for a few sessions of staff inservice training . . . and then wonder why your results fall short of the benchmarked school's. In looking at individual trees, many well-intentioned educators continue to miss the forest—the underlying and universal principles, processes, and practices that drive sustained, continuous improvement of student results.

Savanna Oaks didn't adopt a program, a model, or a specific school design. The staff didn't go looking for a quick fix or a "package" that would answer the challenges they faced in helping students learn. But they did develop their capacity for leading, learning, and change. How they—and many other school staffs like them—did so is the subject of this book.

The Achievement–Learning Connection

Sharing responsibility for student learning may sound like a cliché, but it's very difficult and very rare. In fact, we believe if more schools were actually *doing it*, "forced improvement" through legislated accountability policies would not be necessary. Politicians are responding to the public outcry against poor schooling. This outcry, and the accompanying demand for more accountability, indicates that many U.S. schools are providing students with a subpar educational experience—not all schools, of course, but certainly enough to provoke *national* concern.

Although the standards movement has been instrumental in pushing schools and districts to examine and align what is taught, when it's taught, and why, educators know that standards alone do not improve student learning. And we know that standardized tests are not the sole or even the most meaningful measure of learning. Educators are particularly sensitive to the dangers of extrapolating the meaning of test scores beyond the intended purpose of such measures. Many of us would say that standardized test scores represent a simplistic view of the educational enterprise, and that a too-exclusive focus on test scores threatens to drive all the creativity, passion, and innovation out of our profession.

But consider how educators' arguments against standardized testing must sound to African American, Hispanic, and low-income families: The "achievement gap" for their children has endured for many decades. For these families, it is frustrating at best to hear educators say that standardized tests aren't meaningful, true measures of student learning. Whether or not one "believes in" standardized test scores as a reflection of school quality, in a very real and practical sense, many children—both minority and nonminority—are graduating ill-prepared for a world that values mathematical, technological, and literacy skills.

For better or worse, the public is measuring the "quality" of U.S. schools by standardized test scores—and many schools are not measuring up. If you are a parent facing the decision about where to send your child to school, it's likely you are considering test scores. As Colleen, a parent of pre-kindergarten twins, recently told us, "Our neighborhood school has some of the lowest test scores in the city, and even though it has smaller class sizes now, I'm not sure I want to take a chance."

On the other hand, families also worry that the current emphasis on testing will drive the love of learning right out of their children. Recently, our friend Alan, the father of a kindergartner, bemoaned test-focused instruction, saying, "What if my daughter wants to pursue an interest that doesn't appear on the test? Where is there room for her to enjoy the arts, physical movement, engagement in democratic processes—not just as add-ons, but as part of educating her as a whole child? Is the purpose of schooling just to turn out good test-takers?"

We would suggest that it's not a matter of "either/or" but "both/and." Schools need to focus on helping all students achieve high standards and providing all students well-rounded educational experiences.

Research shows that where there is shared responsibility for student learning, student achievement—for every subgroup—improves (see Barth, Haycock, & Jackson, 1999; Cawelti, 1999; Newmann & Associates, 1996). In schools with cultures of shared responsibility, many of which we highlight in this book, the *purpose* of what they do is not to improve test scores. If that were the case, the staffs would simply align all curricular and instructional practices to "teach to the tests" . . . and eventually discover their test scores hit a plateau and then decrease (Hoff, 2000). Rather, these schools' objective is *to continuously improve student learning;* rising standardized test scores is just one of many important measures of success.

In addition to improved test scores, how else would we measure success in schools where everyone shares responsibility for student learning? We'd look for

• Classroom, school, and district-developed assessments that show steady improvement for every individual and every group of students.

• Increasing rates of student, parent, teacher, and community satisfaction on a variety of indicators important to these constituents.

• Improved efficiencies in the use of resources such as staff development dollars, curriculum choices, staff deployment decisions, and—perhaps most critically—time.

• Evidence of renewed energy for teaching, learning, and leading.

• Students actively engaged and taking responsibility for their learning.

• Deeper, more enduring connections between students, teachers, parents, administrators, and the community.

The list above provides the global indicators of success we believe all schools should strive for. However, each school and district needs to define what it means by "success." Taking the time to do so is integral to the process of building shared responsibility for student learning.

Why Aren't We There Now?

If shared responsibility for student learning is key to student achievement, why aren't there more schools like Savanna Oaks? For all the attention aimed at educational reform over the past decade, you'd think nearly every school would have made progress. But even the most optimistic person would have to admit that there has been little overall improvement in the quality of U.S. public education.

Why is this? It's not for lack of money or desire. State legislatures, the federal government, business and industry, and special interest and community groups have pumped billions of dollars into educational reform. They have spent countless hours in debate and strategy sessions and have added their voices to the groundswell of calls demanding "better education." Neither can we attribute the lack of progress to school systems' inability to change. Recent history has shown schools capable of integrating other massive reforms, such Title I, special education, and Perkins III, all of which arose from state and federal mandates and are financed by public funds. Thanks to several major federal initiatives, schools have significantly changed the kind of education provided to a number of student populations and the kind of material presented within several content areas.

So why haven't we seen more systemic improvement in education? Because public demands and federal mandates can't fundamentally improve the system of teaching and learning that occurs every day, in every classroom, and in every school (O'Neil, 2000). This kind of fundamental reform—*the transformation of the teaching and learning system*—can only come from the inside-out. It must start at the classroom level and move out into the system at large.

Building Capacity for Leadership, Learning, and Change

Think for a moment about what it would take to create shared responsibility for improved student learning at your school.

Teachers and *principals* would need to know best instructional practices. They would have to understand the purpose, role, and value of assessments and data-gathering techniques; use wisdom, commitment, and professional expertise to set results-based goals; and use the data to inform continuous practice improvement.

Classified staff would need to know how to continuously refine and improve noninstructional processes to ensure programs and systems could run efficiently and effectively. They would have to understand their day-to-day influence on the school's children and families. They would need to know how to work collaboratively with teachers and principals to solve problems and get things done.

Students would need to know their individual learning styles, how they learn best, and how to self-assess their skills and capabilities. They would need to understand how to set personal goals that are meaningful and challenging and how to work with others to achieve those goals.

Parents would need to know how to support their children's learning. They would need to understand how to partner effectively with school personnel; how to work with school and community resources to achieve their goals for their children; how to become clear voices in the school's overall vision; and how to help the school accomplish this vision.

As you see, there are many variables involved. And this is the reason why shared responsibility for student learning cannot be accomplished by a piece of legislation, a grant program, a single leader, or a few interested teachers or parents. Rather, shared responsibility must be the work of *leadership* as Linda Lambert defines the term in her book *Building Leadership Capacity in Schools* (1998). Leadership, Lambert tells us, is a concept that is not tied to individuals, official positions, or sets of behavior. Leadership is the school's overall capacity for broad-based, skillful participation in the creation and fulfillment of a vision focused on student learning.

Data coming out of the University of Wisconsin's Center for Education Research support Lambert's views. In research into the potential of professional development activities to improve student achievement in high-poverty, high-achieving schools, Fred Newmann, Bruce King, and Peter Youngs (1999) found that "professional development is more likely to advance achievement of all students in a school if [professional development] addresses not only the learning of individual teachers, but also other dimensions of the organizational capacity of the school" (p. 1). The "organizational capacity" Newmann, King, and Youngs refer to is synonymous with a shared mission, congruent programs, and skillful and broad-based collaboration; all of these are components of what Lambert calls "leadership capacity."

One of the key characteristics of personnel within "high-capacity" schools is that they continuously contribute to each other's learning for the purpose of improving student learning. Consequently, these schools are characterized by an emphasis on building and nurturing relationships within a context of community; creating shared vision and goals; and building educators' skills in the areas of collaboration, inquiry, dialogue, and the application of data to inform decisions and practice.

High-capacity schools also exhibit a strong focus on developing teachers' competence in instruction and assessment within their curricular areas; maintaining program coherence and continuity (avoiding "the fad of the day"); and developing high-quality technical resources, such as curriculum, books, assessment instruments, computers, and workspaces.

Finally, high-capacity schools always have an effective principal—one who positively influences the life of the school and fills what Lambert calls the role of the "formal leader." This is the individual who initiates the dialogue about school vision, maintains the dialogue's focus on teaching and learning, and then creates the time and expectation that staff will collaboratively learn and develop toward that vision (Lambert & Conzemius, 2000).

In this book, we lay the groundwork for building shared responsibility for student learning through a process of continuous personal and organizational learning. Sharing responsibility for student success can and should be applied at every level of the educational organization, whether it's between a classroom teacher and an individual student or between the board and the central office administration. But perhaps the most important place for these conversations to occur is at the school site, where teachers can learn together in community.

A Word About Words

Words are particularly important to educators, and throughout this book we have been very intentional about our word choices. In recent times, the terms "high standard" and "results" have come under heavy fire. We would like to make our position clear at the outset.

• *We strongly support the development and communication of clear, challenging, and consistent standards and expectations by the people who are working most closely with students.* From our perspective, the most important point in the whole standards debate is that educators are using input from parents, community members, and outside research to improve the consistency of the K–12 educational system in their district. Having rational standards that are based on a deep

understanding of child development, important content, and best pedagogical practices is critical to providing high-quality education for all students.

• *Both "processes" and "results" are important.* We believe good processes lead to good results. For far too long, educators have focused solely on processes—activities, innovations, programs, strategies, and so forth—without a concomitant focus on end results. The net effect is that we have left ourselves vulnerable to outsiders telling us which results matter, and now we are stuck with far too many standards and far too much standardized testing. As educators, we need to begin taking responsibility for measuring the effects of the activities and strategies we undertake to improve student learning and achievement so that we know and can communicate what works and what doesn't. This self-reflective ability lies at the heart of "professionalizing" our profession.

• *There is a distinction to be made between student achievement and student learning.* When we refer to "improving student achievement," the assumption we're making is that commercially developed standardized tests are the most frequent measure of achievement (although district-developed assessment tools are becoming more and more popular). When we refer to "improving student learning," we are assuming that "learning" is being measured by a variety of tools, including performance assessments, projects and models, portfolios, and other "authentic" assessments. We also use the term "improving results," by which we mean improving both student learning and achievement.

Making a Difference

How do you know that what you do makes a difference? We took this question to heart as we prepared this book and made a commitment to include only those processes that we know *really work*, either because we've seen their effective application first-hand in schools or because they are supported by academic research and the literature.

In Chapter 1, we present a conceptual framework for building shared responsibility for student learning. Subsequent chapters explore various aspects of that framework in depth and describe how it works in practice. Chapter 2 describes how to achieve shared focus at the school site. Chapter 3 provides an in-depth look at the power of reflection; and Chapter 4 adds the "why and how" of collaboration. Chapter 5 introduces "SMART goals"—the means for powering shared responsibility's continuous personal and organizational learning. Finally, Chapter 6 pulls all the elements together to describe what the leadership capacity created through shared responsibility looks like and feels like in practice.

The true test of whether what we've written will make a difference depends on your ability to create unique meaning from this book in your classroom, school, or district. We encourage you to think of building shared responsibility for student learning as an ongoing activity, and not an end product. It is a journey, not a destination.

Savanna Oaks did not get to where it is overnight. In fact, it has been nearly a decade since that school's principal first asked the teachers to envision the school of their dreams. Those early discussions kicked off an extraordinary amount of critical thinking, strategic planning, and skill building, all of which coalesced to support a school that shows constantly improving levels of student learning.

If the work of building shared responsibility for student learning is a journey, it is not an easy one. There are no quick shortcuts and no simple solutions. Throughout this book, we share stories and insights collected from our interviews with teachers and principals who have embarked on this challenging and rewarding journey. All of them would tell you it is well worth the effort.

1

A Framework for Building
Shared Responsibility

When you start on your journey to Ithaca
then pray that the road is long,
full of adventure, full of knowledge.

—Cavafy, The Poet of Alexandria from "The Journey to Ithaca"

It's 2:00 p.m. at Roosevelt Elementary School* on a Thursday late in April. The 4th grade teachers are gathered around a table, examining data from the most recent schoolwide assessment of student writing. They work undistracted; their district contract calls for "early release" one day a week, and the school planning council has decided to devote this time to collaborative planning and reflection.

On this day, John notes, "My group started out as the highest in writing performance, but made the least amount of gain."

"Why do you think that is?" his colleague asks.

"Maybe that's normal," another suggests.

"No," replies John, "I think it's because I lost focus this quarter. My feedback to the kids was really limited. I spent time on other things. Look at my feedback log. Last quarter I used five different strategies on four different assignments. This quarter, I only gave them written feedback on two assignments, and we only worked on vocabulary in two subject areas."

A fourth colleague offers John some consolation. "Well, don't beat yourself up. Your group still made gains and we have two months to go. What I'm excited about is that it appears our new strategies for giving feedback to our students are really working."

Down the hall, Roosevelt's principal is meeting with two teachers from the Open Classroom program. This program, an integrated, constructivist,

---

*Roosevelt Elementary School, Auburn Hills Intermediate School, and Eagle Ridge Elementary School are all composites of schools and school experiences we have observed.

performance-based learning environment, is the brainchild of three Roosevelt teachers who followed their vision of what they believed school should be like. They designed and piloted the program on a small scale and eventually made it available to all K–5 students.

Now, four years later, one of the three original teachers has left the school, and the two remaining founders, Beth and Mike, are discussing how they would like to work with the departed teacher's replacement.

"Jessie's struggling with the transition," Mike tells the principal.

Beth adds, "Of all the candidates we interviewed, she was the one most on board with the philosophy, but she just hasn't had any experience or training in how to translate it into a different way to teach."

After talking through some of the specifics of Jessie's struggles, Beth and Mike share their plan. "We've figured out a way to schedule time for her to have some collaborative planning and teaching time with each of us, and for us to have some time to observe and mentor her. We've thought through what our budget can handle and are pretty sure that with a few modifications, we can afford to have a part-time aide come in while we are working with Jessie."

"What can I do to help?" the principal asks.

"Stay out of the way!" laughs Mike. "This is an issue for our team to handle and we want to have the chance to work it through together. If we need you, we'll call." The meeting adjourns with encouraging words from the principal.

Later that day, a committee of six students, four teachers, and four parents get together to hold the regular schoolwide climate meeting. The meeting is called to order by a parent, who serves as co-chair with a 3rd grade teacher. Today's agenda focuses on the problem of playground injuries. The committee will be reviewing data from a survey of students, staff, and parents and additional data compiled from interviews with playground supervisors and students who have either been injured or have been referred for disciplinary action related to an injury.

The discussion is lively as the group uses the data to focus on specific causes and locations of injuries. As they examine their graphs, everyone starts talking about interpretations and sharing ideas. A student speaks up to remind the group of its ground rules: "Hey, everyone, one at a time. We've got too many people talking at once. I can't hear."

As the end of the agenda approaches, one of the parents calls for a time check. "We have 10 minutes left," she says, "and we still have to review one more chart and plan our next steps." The co-chairs agree to move on to the last chart, and, with three minutes remaining, the team constructs its next agenda and assigns roles for the next meeting.

Who is responsible for student learning at Roosevelt Elementary School?

A Framework for Shared Responsibility

Let's look at what's going on at Roosevelt. Everyone, from teachers and parents to students and the principal, is working together toward the same goals. Everyone is participating. In short, Roosevelt has achieved shared responsibility—not just for student results, but for *everything* that happens in

1.1	**A Framework for Shared Responsibility**

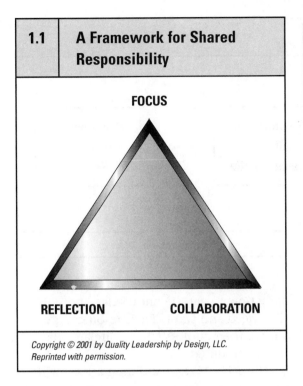

FOCUS

REFLECTION   **COLLABORATION**

Copyright © 2001 by Quality Leadership by Design, LLC.
Reprinted with permission.

the school. How? By building a framework of three elements, as shown in Figure 1.1 (A. Conzemius, 2000).

- *Focus* creates shared clarity of thought, direction, and purpose.
- *Reflection* helps people learn from what they've done in the past and identify better ways of accomplishing their goals.
- *Collaboration* brings people together to share ideas and knowledge.

Together, focus, reflection, and collaboration work to create and shape ongoing improvement. And as Figure 1.2 illustrates, with this framework in place, leadership becomes a matter of shared responsibility, not positional authority.

Each element of the framework relies on the others. Take away one element, and the structure will collapse; it will stand only when all three supports are present and equally strong. Consider these examples:

- A large suburban high school is very clear about its *focus*, which is to prepare a high percentage of students to attend universities and colleges. But because there is no *collaboration* within this school, the same teachers always teach the same college prep courses in isolation from their colleagues, the same portion of students always end up in non-college prep courses, and the same portion of students drop out each year. Further, because no one looks at the data, and no one *reflects* on what it might mean, the school staff is oblivious to this state of affairs.

- An urban elementary school long under fire for lackluster achievement scores has tried to improve test results by providing teachers with training in how to examine students' test data and develop goals for improvement. However, because no time for *collaboration* has been built into teachers' schedules, and no collaborative skills have been promoted through professional development, the teachers rarely get together to use their new data analysis and goal-setting skills. Further, because the school hasn't invested time in nurturing a common *focus*—shared vision, values, and goals—there is tremendous staff resistance to enacting the kinds of changes the data support. The result? Despite an emphasis on *reflection*, there has been no measurable improvement at this school.

- A rural middle school prides itself on its teamwork and "sense of school family." The students are involved in a number of curriculum projects that help develop team skills. Teachers and students work together to resolve the various issues and challenges that come up in the course of the school day. Teachers are also deeply involved in school governance. And yet, despite this strong emphasis on *collaboration*, student achievement lags behind other schools in

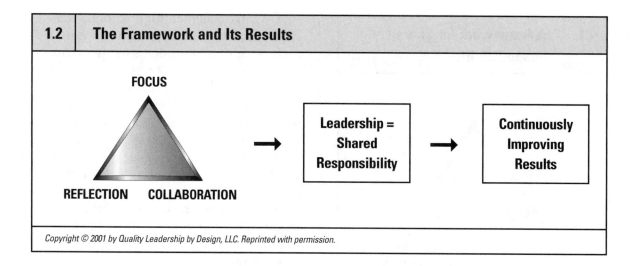

1.2 | **The Framework and Its Results**

FOCUS

REFLECTION   COLLABORATION

Leadership =
Shared
Responsibility

Continuously
Improving
Results

Copyright © 2001 by Quality Leadership by Design, LLC. Reprinted with permission.

the state. Parents have begun to question whether their children are receiving the quality of education they deserve. Lacking focus and refection, the school "feels good," but is it really doing as well as it could?

The schools in these examples are all very committed to one element of the framework but are missing the strength of using the elements in combination. By neglecting the other elements, each school is actually hindering its ability to improve results. The next chapters of this book examine each of the framework's elements in depth and discuss not only the underlying principles of focus, reflection, and collaboration, but also strategies and methods for their implementation. But first, here is a quick overview.

Focus

Children who have been well-nourished physically, emotionally, socially, and cognitively from the very beginning of their lives will usually survive—and perhaps even thrive—despite a mediocre school. Regardless of the approaches their teachers use, these children will learn to read and will learn how to do math. They will learn

early how to get the knowledge and skills they need and want. Their resources are varied; their choices later in life are relatively unlimited.

The schools these children attend will probably look fairly good if the teachers are relatively competent and care about their charges. These are the schools that may not feel the need to create a common focus— the vision, mission, values, and expectations that will lead them to new levels of performance. But schools that skip this step miss an enormous opportunity to create places of learning that are exciting, inspirational, and making a difference for the students and families they serve.

Adlai Stevenson High School illustrates this point. Located in Lincolnshire, Illinois, the school serves 1500 students living in one of Chicago's affluent northern suburbs. Stevenson is ranked as one of the top 50 schools in the Midwest, and given all the advantages students have going in, this is hardly surprising. But back in 1985, things were different. As a graduate from that era told us, "The school was huge, and no one seemed to know what anyone else was doing. Students didn't respect themselves or their teachers. There was no focus. It was rudderless."

When new principal Rick DuFour arrived at Stevenson in 1985, one of his first actions was to lead the school through the process of creating shared vision, mission, and core values, along with clear standards and expectations. By 1992, with results-oriented goals and collaborative team time in place, Stevenson had risen to first in the region according to scores on the college boards. Two years later, it ranked in the top 20 schools in the world. By 1996, Stevenson had broken its own records in average ACT and SAT scores, the percentage of students earning honor grades on advanced placement tests, and average scores in each of the five areas of the state achievement test (DuFour, 1995).

Stevenson's story illustrates the improvement power focus can bring to a school that "has it all," economically speaking. What about high-poverty, traditionally low-achieving schools? At these schools, focus is more than just important to success—it's absolutely vital.

Gordon Cawelti, a longtime educator and now a researcher for Educational Research Service, has made it his life's work to find successful schools serving low-income children and document what has led to their success. He notes that in such schools, "There is a message that permeates the culture of the school that student achievement is important" (Richardson, 2000, p. 6).

Cawelti is describing a school where everyone is focused on the same outcomes. When educators are focused, we have specific outcomes in mind and concentrate on doing those things we think will help us achieve those outcomes (and *not* working on the things that will not contribute). To achieve focus we must clarify, "What is our purpose? What do we want to become?"

The answers to these questions provide the purpose for results we seek and the answers to the "so what?" and "why" of what we do.

Working toward a common focus helps a school separate its daily urgent issues from the important priorities it must nurture on a longer-term basis. Focus helps everyone stay centered on the common purpose. Focus is also about aligning and communicating clear goals, expectations, and standards. The power of designing curriculum, instruction, assessment, and teacher evaluation that link to standards is evidenced by Education Trust's 1999 study of high-performing, high-poverty schools. The organization's 1999 report, edited by Barth, Haycock, and Jackson and titled *Dispelling the Myth: High Poverty Schools Exceeding Expectations,* details the characteristics of 366 urban and rural schools that meet two general criteria: All have poverty levels exceeding 50 percent and all have been identified by their states as high performing and/or most improving. Here are some of the study's most significant findings:

• 80 percent of the 366 schools reported using standards to design curriculum and instruction.

• 94 percent reported using standards to assess student progress.

• 77 percent had developed ways to help teachers assess student work against state standards (Barth, Haycock, & Jackson, 1999, p. 4).

The manner in which a school implements standards speaks to that school's understanding of the standards-based movement as a part of a process of continuous learning and improvement. In schools making progress, significant resources go toward giving teachers time to work together to develop curriculum and instructional approaches that are aligned with the state standards. What does this process look like in practice? Throughout the year, teachers meet regularly to review their curricular units for thematic integrity; evaluate students' progress on district-developed assessments; develop skills-based, flexible groupings; and share instructional approaches and strategies. At the end of each year, the full faculty reviews state test results, summarizes what students appear to have learned, and celebrates progress toward schoolwide goals. Then, at the beginning of the new school year, the faculty meets again to reexamine their instructional strategies and programmatic results and to develop or refine their schoolwide goals.

Although a school's focus shouldn't change with every whim, it can't be set in concrete either. At Roosevelt Elementary School, the faculty, staff, and students continually assess their focus, based on their continuous learning. "Where do we want to be?" they ask. "Are the answers we gave before still valid? What is most important to help us get there? What do we believe?" As demonstrated in the case study at the beginning of this chapter, such questions permeate conversations at every level of the Roosevelt community:

• "Why do you think [your group has made the least amount of gain]?" "I think it's because *I lost my focus* this quarter. My feedback to the kids was really limited. I spent time on other things."

• "Of all the candidates we interviewed, she was the one *most on board with the philosophy . . . .*"

• The discussion is lively as the group *uses the data to focus* on specific causes and locations of injuries.

In short, a shared, unwavering commitment to the clear vision and goal of improving student results is a key difference between schools that are succeeding and those that are failing or are simply mediocre.

Reflection

Another key ingredient in Roosevelt's success is the school's emphasis on taking the time to evaluate current performance, using data as much as possible. The questions that promote *reflection* include "Where are we now?" "How well are we doing compared to what we want to accomplish?" and "What are we learning?"

Reflection helps educators go beyond best guesses or informed hunches about what is and is not working. If our objective is to make real improvements in our schools' systems of learning, our own classroom practices, and our personal and interpersonal effectiveness, we need to solicit and use feedback—both hard numbers and subjective perceptions.

Reflection has a powerful ability to create change when it is applied at the personal level. Alan Groth, an elementary school principal with whom we've worked, adapted a comment from Bonhoeffer (1954) to develop his own method of keeping on track: "At the end of every day, I sit back and reflect on what I have done as a principal to facilitate the success of this process. I ask myself, have I made teachers free, strong and mature . . . or weak and dependent?"

Students' ability to reflect on their learning and make adjustments accordingly has been identified as one of the most significant determinants of student success. The Mid-Atlantic Regional Lab conducted a meta-analysis of more than 11,000 statistical findings correlating school factors with achievement (Wang, Haertel, & Walberg, 1994). According to this study, students' metacognitive processes (planning, monitoring the effectiveness of attempted actions and outcomes, and testing, revising, and evaluating learning strategies) had an influence on learning second only to teachers' ability to maintain active student participation.

Further, in a study of 26 high-achieving, high-poverty schools in Texas, researchers identified teachers' ability to accurately identify student needs—through the use of assessments and other "reflection" tools—and to plan instruction accordingly, as a common characteristic of successful classrooms (Johnson, 1998). The researchers found that

> Teachers were attuned to the special ways in which individual students learned best. They exploited this knowledge to create learning environments that allowed many students to attain challenging academic skills. Formative assessments allowed teachers to accurately determine areas of strength and need, participate in the planning and delivery of professional development, and contribute to decisions about the use of other resources (pp. 3–4).

At Roosevelt Elementary School, reflective practices are in evidence everywhere you look:

• The 4th grade teachers are . . . *examining data* from the most recent schoolwide assessment of student writing.

• "Look at my *feedback log.* Last quarter I used five different strategies on four different assignments. This quarter, I only gave them written feedback on two assignments and we only worked on vocabulary in two subject areas."

• The Open Classroom program . . . is the brainchild of three Roosevelt teachers who . . . *designed and piloted the program on a small scale* and eventually made it available to all K–5 students.

• The committee will be *reviewing data from a survey* of students, staff, and parents and *additional data from interviews* with playground supervisors and students who have either been injured or have been referred for disciplinary action related to an injury.

Staff reflection can also benefit students in an indirect way. In a review of the literature on teacher efficacy and achievement, Tschannen-Moran, Woolfolk Hoy, and Hoy (1998) found "the perception that a performance has been successful raises efficacy beliefs, which contributes to the expectation of proficient performance in the future" (p. 229). In practical terms, this means teachers will have more confidence in their teaching methods and approaches if they gather data on their own students' performance and use the data to confirm effective practices and uncover ineffective ones. No wonder that we've observed the greatest sense of focus, direction, and vibrant energy residing in classrooms where the teachers (1) purposefully and intentionally link their plans to standards, expectations, and goals; (2) review their student performance each day and week through classroom-based assessments and personal observations; and (3) constantly make instructional improvements based on these reflections.

In summary, reflection is as much a mindset as it is a process, or a set of tools or methods. Reflection is a way of thinking about the world and one's relationship to it. It is the willingness to change because of what the data reveal and the skill to know what to do with the data collected.

Collaboration

Collaboration is the process of developing interdependent relationships where all are focused on a common purpose and set of goals and where people must rely on each other to achieve these goals. It is the synergy created when a group's effectiveness exceeds what individuals can accomplish on their own.

Collaboration doesn't just mean staff members feeling good about each other or liking each other. It is about creating an environment—through structures, systems, processes, and policies—where everyone contributes skills, knowledge, and experience to continuously improve student learning.

Collaboration also extends beyond the school's walls to everyone who can contribute to the school's success. It involves multiple stakeholders: teachers, support staff, administrators, parents, students, and community members. Lambert (1998) characterizes collaboration as "broad-based participation in the work of leadership," and identifies it as a key dimension of successful schools (p. 17). She also observes that within successful schools, the kind of learning that takes place is founded in relationships:

> All of the learning must be embedded in a trusting environment in which relationships form a safety net of support and positive challenge . . . it means that people are in relationship with one another. To be in authentic relationship means that we provide long-term support for one another, challenging one another to improve and to question our current perceptions, and to learn together (Lambert, 1998, p. 16).

In Roosevelt's example, collaboration is *the* way of doing school:

• The 4th grade teachers are gathered around a table, examining data from the most recent schoolwide assessment of student writing. They work undistracted; *their district contract calls for "early release" one day a week,* and *the school planning council has decided to devote this time to collaborative planning and reflection.*

• In their meeting with the principal about their newer colleague, the two experienced Open Classroom teachers claim, *"We've figured out a way to schedule time for her to have some collaborative planning and teaching time with each of us* and for us to have some time to observe and mentor her."

• A committee of six students, four teachers, and four parents get together to hold the regular schoolwide climate meeting. The meeting is called to order by *a parent who serves as co-chair with a 3rd grade teacher. A student speaks up to remind the group of its ground rules. One of the parents calls for a time check. The team constructs its next agenda and assigns roles for the next meeting.*

Collaboration is not easy. Every school and district has its share of the interesting "messiness of humanity," and sometimes this messiness can overwhelm attempts to achieve an ideal of collaborative harmony and productivity. Still, it's the process of trying to work together that enables stakeholders to build a strong foundation of collaboration and learning. In successful schools like Roosevelt, the vision of a collaborative environment where all are learners and all are leaders provides momentum for the journey towards shared responsibility and continuous improvement.

Putting the Pieces Together

In their 1999 research into why some schools use professional development more effectively than others, Newmann, King, and Youngs of the Wisconsin Center for Education Research identified schoolwide *professional community* as a key element of school capacity. They observed that "A strong school professional community consists of (a) the staff sharing clear goals for student learning, (b) collaboration and collective responsibility among staff to achieve the goals, (c) professional inquiry by the staff to address the challenges they face, and (d) opportunities for staff to influence the school's activities and policies" (p. 4).

These researchers go on to note that studies have shown a clear link between strong professional community and higher student achievement. The factors they cite—shared goals, collaboration and collective responsibility, and professional inquiry—combine to create the synergy of our framework for shared responsibility:

- "Shared goals" arise from work on achieving focus.
- "Collaboration and collective responsibility" include teams of teachers coming together to focus on student learning goals.
- "Professional inquiry" involves reflection on data about what students are learning.

Together, these factors give schools and teachers the tools they need to develop and sustain methods for improving curriculum and instruction in a continuous improvement cycle.

In schools that have high capacity, King and Newmann (2000) found "strong individual staff competence directed toward focused and sustained collective purposes and supported through reflective collaboration and empowerment of the full staff" (p. 578). This description sounds very much like Roosevelt and the framework that Roosevelt has put in place to develop shared responsibility for student learning. In the next three chapters, we look at focus, collaboration, and reflection in greater depth and emphasize what it takes to establish and sustain each.

It took Roosevelt Elementary School more than half a decade to progress from the very first whispers about change to the widespread implementation of far-reaching improvements. But in the minds of everyone in the school community, the payoff is well worth the effort invested in the journey; today, everyone at Roosevelt knows the answer to the question, "Who's responsible for student learning?"

The answer: "I am."

2 Focus

I am an advocate for children. This filters everything I do, every decision I make, every action I take.

SANDY GUNDERSON, PRINCIPAL, MENDOTA ELEMENTARY SCHOOL
MADISON, WISCONSIN

When new principal Sandy Gunderson arrived at Mendota Elementary in the fall of 1998, the school had been in distress for a number of years. Student achievement was down, union grievances were common, and parents were choosing to send their children elsewhere. Seven interim principals had come and gone within three years.

One of the first students the new principal met was Anthony, a boy who spent the greater part of each day in the office, having been ejected from his classrooms. At the first full faculty meeting, Sandy called on the staff to work with her to meet a higher standard. "I want us to create a school where Anthony will succeed," she told them. "I'd like to see every one of us focusing our efforts on ensuring that he does not fail. And as we learn how to work together to help Anthony succeed, *all* our students will succeed. No child—including Anthony—will fall through the cracks."

Two years later, a local newspaper headline trumpeted, "Mendota School does a 180! Turnaround draws bravos!" (Murphy, 2000). Mendota is now among the highest performing elementary schools in the district—in spite of high poverty and former low achievement. Jill Jokela, the president of Mendota's PTO, comments on the changes and the school's new climate:

> When Sandy came in, she got everybody on the same page and helped us set higher expectations for the students. We formed a steering committee with a vision and plan for what we wanted things to look like. The school now is a great place. We have technology that's integrated into the curriculum. The curriculum is aligned. We have smaller classes in the lower grades. Kids are learning faster. We instituted better and more communication with families. Before, individual teachers were good but

18

isolated from each other. Now everyone works together. Everything's fallen into place. It's amazing.

If you visit Mendota today, you will find yourself in a safe, calm, creative school where everyone is learning—both children and adults. You will see teachers, administrators, and staff who demonstrate an intense *focus* in all they do. This focus has come about through many hours spent articulating and refining their values, vision, mission, and goals. The team at Mendota will tell you that their focusing work is never "done" and put on a shelf; rather, they use the clarity their focus gives them to filter and prioritize everything they do.

Mendota Elementary serves as a strong example of how focus can help turn around a low-performing school. If you need additional evidence that organizing schools around a clear, shared sense of mission makes a difference in student learning, Newmann and Wehlage's 1995 longitudinal study of more than 1400 schools certainly provides it. They observed what can happen in the *absence* of such a sense of purpose: "When schools are unable to coordinate teachers' diverse aims for students into a curricular mission focused on high-quality student learning, it is difficult for even the most gifted teachers to make a positive difference for students" (p. 2).

This chapter describes how schools and districts can develop powerful focus by reaching consensus on values, vision, mission, and strategic priorities. Later, in Chapter 5, we will show how you can use "SMART" goals—goals that are *S*pecific and *S*trategic, *M*easurable, *A*ttainable, *R*esults-oriented, and *T*imebound (O'Neill,

2000a)—to sharpen the focus of your school's strategic improvement efforts.

Before we go any further, let's pause here to reiterate what focus is and where it resides. When we talk about *focus,* we're talking about shared goals, values, mission, and vision. These elements are needed at every "altitude" of the educational system. Focus is essential at all levels—classroom, school, and district—and throughout all operations.

Unfortunately, many schools and districts either discount or minimize the value of focus. Some of the comments we've heard include, "We don't need to spend time developing mission, values, and vision—we need to improve our test scores!" and "We did that six years ago. Where did I put that plan?" Another is, "We believe in lifelong learning. Is that what you mean?" In the following sections, we explain the group processes we have used to help individual schools and school districts establish clear focus—the foundation on which all improvement is built.

Elements of Focus

In his book *The Fifth Discipline* (1990), noted author, lecturer, and organizational researcher Peter Senge writes, "One is hard pressed to think of any organization that has sustained some measure of greatness in the absence of goals, values, and missions that become deeply shared throughout the organization" (p. 9). Goals, values, missions—and vision—are what help keep educational organizations focused on the critical factors that will determine whether students succeed or fail. Each of these elements is important, and any district or school committed to building shared responsibility for student success must address them all.

In the corporate world, you'll often hear people talk about the importance of starting with a mission statement; however, because education is already such a mission-driven, service-minded endeavor, we advise schools and school districts to begin their quest for focus with an examination of their core values, and then move from these into the development of shared vision. Starting from core values allows each person to speak from personal convictions; when we begin with the personal and move outward to the communal group, we can ensure that each person sees his or her place in the resulting vision.

Core Values and Beliefs

The importance of setting aside time to understand and reach agreement on core values and beliefs cannot be overstated. When Newmann and Wehlage (1995) investigated the cause-and-effect relationship between school restructuring strategies and student achievement, they examined the relative effectiveness of the following tools and approaches: shared decision making, school choice, schools within schools, flexible scheduling and longer classes, team teaching, common academic curriculum, external standards, reduction of ability grouping and tracking, and new forms of assessment. Their findings were surprising: The effectiveness of each of these improvement strategies "depends on how well it organizes or develops *the values, beliefs,* and technical skills of educators to improve student learning" (p. 1, emphasis ours).

Patricia Wasley, Robert Hampel, and Richard Clark (1997) at New York's Bank Street College agree with this assessment. They cite a number of factors as essential for successful whole school reform, among

them the staff's ability to deal directly with difficult and often-controversial issues, receive and act on critical feedback from external sources, and understand school culture issues. All these factors have to do with core values—who we are as a school, how we deal with issues, what we believe, and how we act as a consequence.

People sometimes use the terms "beliefs" and "values" interchangeably, but there is a practical difference. *Belief* statements are expressions of what we believe to be true about a particular topic, issue or group; they express our underlying assumptions, are often subconscious, may be implicit in what we say, and require dialogue to be made explicit. Beliefs frequently reflect our core values; they are powerful shapers of how we think and choose to act.

A *core value* is an enduring principle or a deeply held commitment that drives the conduct of the organization. Leaders rely on core values to guide their decision making, their priorities, and their actions. When we are living and working according to our core values, and when these core values drive our vision and mission, there is alignment, direction, and energy within the school. If our values are truly the driving force behind our actions, school visitors will see them at work. Our core values are behaviorally anchored and they are observable. Let's take a closer look at how beliefs and values influence the direction and decisions of school communities.

Beliefs

Beliefs can have a profound influence on the educational climate school staffs create for their students and themselves. Educators and authors Jon Saphier and John D'Auria (1993) write, "The behaviors of

2.1	Liberating and Limiting Beliefs	
Life-Liberating Beliefs		**Life-Limiting Beliefs**
1. All children are capable of high achievement, not just the fastest and most confident.		1. Only the few and the bright can achieve at a high level.
2. You are not supposed to understand everything the first time around.		2. Speed is what counts. Faster is smarter.
3. Consistent effort is the main determinant of success.		3. Inborn intelligence is the main determinant of success.
4. Mistakes help one learn.		4. Mistakes are a sign of weakness.
5. Good students work together and solicit help from one another.		5. Competition is necessary to bring out the best in our students.

Adapted by permission of the publisher from How to Bring Vision to School Improvement *by Jon Saphier and John D'Auria. Copyright © 1993 Research for Better Teaching.*

parents and staff toward children in instructional situations stem from beliefs . . . those beliefs dramatically influence what we do with children and how open children are to learning" (p. 10).

Figure 2.1 contrasts what Saphier and D'Auria call "life-liberating" and "life-limiting" beliefs and highlights just how critical educators' beliefs can be. Consider the very different school environments that would arise from these disparate outlooks. School community members must make the time to dialogue about beliefs and values so they can shape a vision that is meaningful and will guide their future actions.

Core Values

According to Saphier and D'Auria (1993), core values come from "thinking about ourselves and how we would need to interact to be an effective organization" (p. 8). To

put it another way, core values are commitments to how a school's staff will operate internally.

For example, one rural school district we worked with developed core values as part of its strategic planning process. Early in the process, teachers, administrators, staff, parents, and board and community members came together to explore the kind of learning climate they needed to create in order to ensure the success of their strategic initiatives. After a series of lively meetings, the district stakeholders were able to express their core values in the following key statements:

• We treat each individual as we wish to be treated—with trust, respect, and dignity.

• When we make mistakes, we honor the learning opportunity. When we err, we forgive.

• No one person can know or do everything. We operate with mutual collegiality, interdependence, and in an atmosphere of experimentation.

• Relationships count more than structures, position descriptions, titles, and functions.

This district's organizational effectiveness had long been stymied by fear and mistrust. In the past, when unintentional errors by administrators, teachers, or staff had been discovered, the culture supported efforts to publicly shame the person, most often through the use of written memos with long "cc:" lists.

Once the district's core values emerged, personnel began frank, lengthy, and sometimes painful conversations about "how things are around here." People began to look to these core values to suggest new ways to react to mistakes, errors, and "bad news." Today, this district is a healthier and more open place to work and learn in, thanks to the work undertaken to clarify core values and the commitment of courageous individuals who continue to speak up when folks lapse into old behaviors. People are working hard to create more trusting, positive, life-liberating relationships, and they continue to look to their core values as a guide for daily behavior.

Saphier and D'Auria (1993) also suggest that core values be generated around big picture student outcomes—the "things learned by students that change them as people" (p. 7). Their description of outcome-focused core values includes the following examples:

• Our students graduate knowing how to ask good questions and find their own answers.

• Our students graduate knowing group skills and how to cooperate and function effectively with others.

• Our students graduate knowing how to apply technology in a changing world.

Core values and beliefs are closely linked. In fact, it's often easiest to develop core value statements from belief statements. Core value statements express "how we'll know we're walking the talk of our beliefs." This is clearly expressed in Figure 2.2's excerpts from the Madison Metropolitan School District's Strategic Plan 2005.

2.2	**Excerpts from the Madison Metropolitan School District's Strategic Plan 2005**

Beliefs
1. Every child has a capacity to learn.
2. Families influence children and society.
3. Schools should enhance learning.
4. Diversity enriches life and learning.

Core Values
We commit ourselves to . . .

1. Offer a challenging, multicultural curriculum that engages students.
   • Work to meet the needs of every individual child.
   • Provide programs and instructional methods that develop children's skills in communication, technology, science, problem solving, thinking, and creativity.
   • Respect the dignity of others.
   • Foster an appreciation of our diverse, democratic society.
   • Actively solicit input and feedback from administration, teachers, staff, parents, students, and community members.
   • Coordinate services with community partners.
2. Support our mission and priorities with resources.

Reprinted by permission of the Madison Metropolitan School District, Madison, Wisconsin. Board members and administrators developed these beliefs and core values as part of their strategic planning process.

Mission

Much research supports the connection between a clear mission and school effectiveness (see Peterson & Warren, 1994). We would argue that being clear about school mission is probably more important today than it's ever been. More and more families are making choices about where (or even if) to enroll their children in public schools. With the options of charter schools, alternate programs, vouchers, and home schooling, a school's mission statement is as much a marketing communications strategy as it is a philosophical "true north." But having a *clear* mission is not enough. A mission statement must also be compelling—it should live in the hearts and minds of the teachers, staff, parents, administrators, and students because it is the raison d'etre—the reason they choose to work in, learn in, and send their children to *this* particular school.

The mission of public education, at least in the ideal, is *to provide all children equal opportunity and access to quality schooling.* However, this kind of traditional mission statement does little to inform families about what makes a particular school unique and worthy of choice. Nor does a statement like this one address the needs of the information age, our global economy, and the multicultural diversity we experience at work and in our communities.

Today, the public expects public schools to educate *all* children and help all reach high standards of achievement. Schools are expected not only to teach students to master basics skills, but also to make them knowledgeable consumers and users of information, collaborative team players, good problem solvers and critical thinkers, and informed, involved community citizens. This is far different from the task of public schools 100 years ago, when completing an 8th grade education in the 3R's was considered the maximum standard needed for the industrial world of work. Additionally, today's rich diversity of students challenges schools to address a much broader range of skills, talents, interests, and abilities, while the growth of dual income and single parent households means less parental support and involvement after school hours.

Thinking About Mission

Rick DuFour, now the superintendent of Adlai Stevenson High School District, provides a powerful way of thinking about the importance of mission. He suggests we take mission statements beyond the platitudes of "all children can learn" and "developing lifelong learners," and push ourselves to describe *what exactly* we expect all children to learn, and how we will respond when all of them *don't* learn (DuFour & Eaker, 1998). He illustrates this with the four statements in Figure 2.3.

These statements express four different instructional positions based on four schools' underlying beliefs about their purpose. It's clear that each of these schools would provide very different experiences for students. For example, the first three statements suggest environments where at least some students would be *expected* to fail. The first statement expresses a belief in ability tracking. The second reveals a school that is willing to give struggling students a little extra assistance, but also anticipates that many of these students will "choose" to fail, regardless. The third statement indicates a school that would make self-esteem building programs and strategies a regular occurrence, but would also accept that some students will continue to fail because "it wouldn't be fair to them to expect more."

2.3	Four Different Belief Statements

Statement 1: **We believe all students can learn . . . *based on their ability.***
Belief: It is our job to create multiple programs or tracks that address these differences in ability... and then to guide students to the appropriate program.

Statement 2: **We believe all students can learn . . . *if they take advantage of the opportunity to learn.***
Belief: Students can learn if they choose to put forth the effort to do so. It is our job to teach; it is the students' job to learn.

Statement 3: **We believe all students can learn . . . *and we will accept responsibility for ensuring their growth.***
Belief: The extent of [a student's] growth will be determined by a combination of the student's innate ability and effort. It is our job to create a warm, inviting classroom climate and to encourage all students to learn as much as possible, but the extent of their learning depends on factors over which we have little control. . . .

Statement 4: **We believe all students can learn . . . *and we will establish high standards of learning that we expect all students to achieve.***
Belief: It is our job to create an environment in our classrooms that engages students in academic work that results in a high level of achievement. . . . We are prepared to work collaboratively with colleagues, students, and parents to achieve this shared educational purpose.

Adapted by permission of the publisher from Professional Learning Communities at Work: Best Practices for Enhancing Student Achievement. *Copyright © 1998 by the National Education Service, 304 West Kirkwood Avenue, Bloomington, IN 47404. Phone: 800-733-6786. Web: www.nesonline.com.*

The fourth statement is the only one that suggests a school where all students really would succeed. It indicates a school where teachers not only recognize the connection between uniform high expectations and success, but also receive the support required to adjust the system of instruction to meet diverse student needs. Only by first understanding and then challenging the first three sets of beliefs will schools begin to come to terms with what's really involved in improving student learning across the board.

Developing a Powerful Mission Statement

A mission statement should describe, briefly and to the point, exactly what purpose the school or district serves, who it serves, and how it delivers those services—in today's terms and based on the particular school community's values and ideals.

Given what we know now about the connection between maintaining high standards for all students and what it takes to help them achieve those standards, we can see that it is *vital* for schools and districts to engage in belief-based mission development at a very deep level, allowing people to voice and come to mutual understandings about their underlying attitudes and assumptions about learning (see Barth, Haycock, & Jackson, 1999; Cawelti, 1999; Newmann & Wehlage, 1995).

Verona Area School District did just that. This district, which educates children from some of the county's poorest and richest families, devoted significant time and effort to mission statement development. Administrators, the board, community members, parents, and school staff took the time to develop a *focus* that all could rally around. The various stakeholders gathered together and worked through their differences, using dialogue as a consensus building process. Here is the mission statement they finally agreed upon:

> The Verona Area School District, a community of learners, values and supports educational excellence. To foster the joy of learning and to prepare students for future challenges, we set rigorous academic and creative expectations for each student. Students, in turn, must show they meet these expectations.

Mission in Action

Because the Verona Area School District values and supports families having educational choices for their children, it provides a variety of different programs and curriculums within its schools and is on the forefront of the Wisconsin Charter School movement. There's no better place to see Verona's mission in action than in the various programs—and program missions—that exist side-by-side at Savanna Oaks Elementary School. The school itself has a mission; the multi-age program that resides within the school has a separate program mission; and the Core Knowledge Charter School, which happens to be located within the same building, has a mission of its own. In Figure 2.4, we've provided the mission statements of the three "programs" that coexist within Savanna Oaks.

These three statements of educational purpose give parents insight into each program and allow them to choose the learning environment that's best for their children. Teachers, too, are drawn to a particular school or program because of its mission. Each mission statement translates into a distinctly different classroom climate. An article in the local newspaper (Carleton, 1996) captured some of the differences between the classrooms operating under each mission and program at Savannah Oaks.

2.4	**Three Missions in One School**

Savanna Oaks Overall Mission
Our mission as a school community is to challenge our students to reach their academic potential, to love and respect them for who they are, and to teach them the absolute joy of learning.

Multi-Age Program Mission
(excerpted from philosophy statement)
Within our community of learners, children engage in hands-on, developmentally appropriate activities and are given numerous opportunities to interact and communicate with peers and adults. Teachers and parents are partners in facilitating and fostering each child's education.

Core Knowledge Charter School Mission
The Core Knowledge Charter School will be a public education option for parents and teachers in the Verona Area School District, where students will develop strong learning skills and a broad base of knowledge through the use of proven educational materials and programs in a safe and structured environment.

Courtesy of Verona Area School District, Verona, Wisconsin.

• At the *Core Knowledge Charter School*, where direct instruction is a key teaching strategy, the reporter noted, "Younger children, such as those in Martha Embling's kindergarten class, seem enthralled by the fast-paced, rhythmic exercises and their teacher's sing-song tones."[*]

• In Savanna Oaks' *traditional classrooms*, teachers share a set of curriculum

---

[*]All quoted material in this section is from G. Carleton. (1996, November 30). Three schools in one. *The Capital Times* (Madison, WI), p. A3.

guidelines, but teach their lessons in very different ways. You might find, as the newspaper reporter did, a teacher whose style is "electric, irreverent and as much game show host as teacher."

• Savanna Oaks' *multi-age program* is housed in another wing of the building: "Its wall folded back, (Paula) Wick's classroom invites children to explore—to choose books from packed shelves, to work on art projects, to sprawl on pillows and write."

These excerpts show Savanna Oaks' three missions in action. For example, the Core Knowledge Charter School's mission includes developing students "in a safe and structured environment." The students in Martha Embling's class are experiencing safety and structure—exactly what their parents value and want for their children. The students in the school's traditional program are experiencing some of the "absolute joy of learning,"—exactly what the program's mission statement aims for. One parent quoted in the article commented that he liked the way the traditional public schools have moved toward an emphasis on problem solving and away from memorization. Meanwhile, the students in the multi-age program are clearly "given numerous opportunities to interact with peers and adults." A parent in this program said she appreciated the teachers' attentiveness to her child, and the fact that her child will be with the same group of children for several years.

The newspaper article goes on to quote Tom Stefonik, Division Director of Instructional Services for Wisconsin's Department of Public Instruction. Summing up the power of offering "three schools in one," Stefonik said, "The 'school within a school' provides something different for the community, but doesn't require total conversion of the public school system to a particular

philosophy." Families' ability to select a particular "school" within their school because of its mission is at the heart of the movement within public education to meet individual needs and family preferences.

It is up to the members of each school community to determine what is most important to them and to develop a corresponding mission. In Chapter 4, we introduce *dialogue* as a process for facilitating deep-level conversations. We encourage schools and districts to engage in this process to arrive at their values, mission, and vision.

Vision

Shared vision provides guidance when times get tough. When enrollment falls, a safety crisis occurs, contract talks stall, or test scores decline, shared vision can minimize the frequency and intensity of conflict, maintain lines of communication, and prevent factions and isolationism from becoming the norm.

For staff at district and school levels, creating shared vision is both a process of ongoing, daily conversation and the result of hard work to define exactly where they would eventually like to be as an organization. A vision is an inspirational picture of the desired future. It is a promise: a commitment to the students, staff, and community.

Here are some of the features of a compelling vision:

• It expresses a belief in a future that is fundamentally better than the current situation.

• It has a clear time frame—at least five years out.

• It helps the school community rise above daily worries and irritations.

• It elevates the school community and helps all members feel that they are contributing to something truly worthy and worthwhile.

- It springs from core values and beliefs.
- It is clear and articulate.
- It is inclusive enough to allow each member of the community to find him or herself in it and serves as a "true north" reference point in conversations about the school.

The best visions have the power to move people emotionally and cognitively. They act as a filter for every decision made, from the classroom to the boardroom. These are the visions that emerge from a process involving key stakeholders who are given time to dream, explore, and think creatively about what is *possible* within a school or district, rather than just what is probable. When faculty, staff, parents, community members, and even students engage together in deep dialogue about their hopes and dreams and their underlying beliefs and values, what emerges is a description of *the community's* preferred future. This vision is based on a solid foundation of shared understanding and has the momentum necessary to sustain change.

The Visioning Process

Writing a vision statement is not what creates successful districts and schools. A school's vision is a living thing, and it's kept alive by the way that everyone in the school community frames each and every conversation. Senge (1990) makes a strong case for going far beyond simply developing a vision statement. He talks about the value of creating shared vision in a dynamic, living process: "Visions that are genuinely shared require ongoing conversation where individuals not only feel free to express their dreams, but learn how to listen to each others' dreams" (p. 218).

At a recent districtwide goal setting meeting we attended, one teacher ("Teacher #1" in the conversation below) protested, "It's not fair to expect *all* children to be proficient. My job is to help each child reach his or her potential." The ensuing conversation, although respectful of this teacher's views, was animated and enlightening. Here are some excerpts:

> *Parent:* I don't know that I'm comfortable going there. I mean, what if it's my child who's graduating—and he's not proficient in some area?

> *Teacher #2:* I can understand that we want to be developmentally appropriate in our approach to working with kids. However, I don't think any one of us is in the position to know what each child's potential really is. There have been plenty of times when my students have surprised me by what they knew and were able to do.

> *Superintendent:* I think the danger here is that if we lower the bar by saying we expect some students won't be proficient, we give up on them—and on our ability to change what we're doing to help them reach higher standards.

> *Principal:* That's really what it comes down to, isn't it? Whether we feel we're competent and able to help all kids reach proficiency?

> *Teacher #1:* I hate to admit it, but that's underlying a lot of why I'm feeling nervous about this vision of proficiency for all kids. I'm not sure, even after years of teaching, that I know how to do that.

This conversation helped unearth deep-seated critical issues that fueled some of the teachers' "resistance" to the district's vision. It took courage for Teacher #1 to speak up about her beliefs and then to admit her fear; this openness was possible because the district's culture (established through both day-to-day interaction and official policies) welcomes inquiry and honest dialogue. The exchange you've just read led this district-level improvement group to focus staff development on increasing teachers' skills and abilities to differentiate instruction, meet the varying needs of students in their efforts, and improve student achievement overall.

Setting the Stage for Creative Visioning

When a school begins the visioning process, it is important for everyone to think about the school's future as something potentially quite different from today's reality. The key is to provide the opportunities, time, and structures people need to talk openly about their hopes and dreams.

There are a number of tools schools and districts can use to help create a shared vision. The best ones keep participants focused on a key question, involve a mix of stakeholders, and build-in time for both large-group and small-group discussions. And although there is no set rule about how many people to involve in the visioning process, the key is to include those who will be in a position to lead or influence others; those who think "out of the box" and bring fresh perspectives; and those who are highly regarded by their peers. We suggest involving individuals from the following stakeholder groups: parent/families, community members, board members, principals, central office administrators, teachers, and other school staff. If possible, also consider involving students, including graduates.

Once the stakeholders have assembled, creating an initial vision statement might take anywhere from four hours to a day or two, depending on the process selected and the numbers of people involved. Some useful meeting aides to have handy at any visioning session include flipcharts, sticky notes, sticky dots, markers, and tape. Typically, sessions begin with a facilitator or leader setting the context and providing the focus question. Individuals then spend a few minutes collecting their thoughts and ideas about the vision before sharing them in a small-group format. A volunteer from each small group records the group's ideas on flipcharts, and the group discusses each idea thoroughly before sharing highlights with the larger group.

One sharing technique that works particularly well in the small-group/large-group format is a "Walkabout." After all the small groups have created their individual vision statements, they post the statements on the walls of the meeting room. Everyone walks about the room, silently reading these ideas and providing feedback by writing comments on sticky notes and attaching them to the flipchart pages. The small groups then return to their statements, read through the comments, and incorporate any changes they would like to make. Following the session, a design team writes a draft of the group's collective thinking, based on the small groups' work. This draft is circulated to both session participants and members of the school community who did not attend the visioning session—all are invited to add their comments.

The following examples show different vision design tools you can use to generate a creative vision statement:

Blue Sky Scenarios.
Ignore all that was or is and work toward creating something totally new. Kick off the discussion with this question: "If we could create the school of our dreams, what would it look like? If our school were doing the best job possible, what would be in place three to five years from now?"

Forecasting Scenarios.

Analyze current trends, make predictions about what the future will bring, and design a vision around these predictions. Begin by asking, "What are the big trends in education? What impact will technology have? Standards-based reforms? The accountability movement? What will be happening with our financial resources in the future? Our human resources? Our demographics?" Working from the same set of data, each group develops separate scenarios and shares them with each other. Use the "best of" and the "most likely" elements from each to craft a vision statement of where you want your school to be.

Time Warp Scenarios.

Imagine you are taking a trip through time that will put you in the future 5 to 10 years from now. You turn on the local news to find a story about your school. Begin the dialogue with this question: "What will we be proud to hear them saying?" Alternately, you emerge from the time warp to find your school has received the Baldrige Award for Educational Excellence, which is given to only a select few schools in the nation. Visitors from all over United States are coming to your school to learn what is going on to make it such an outstanding place. Begin with: "What is our award-winning, model school like? What does it look like? What is happening with students? Staff? Parents? Community?"

Mapping.

Map out the assets of your school and show how each relates to the others. Start the conversation with: "What are our human assets? Our technology assets? Our financial assets? Our geographic assets? What emerges as natural connections? Which needed connections are missing?"

Role-Play.

Rather than just report on visions of the future, groups might choose to write and deliver skits that depict what life in the school could be like.

Any of the designs described above could be used during planned staff development time. We highly recommend any of them as an important and significant way to use this time.

Moving Forward While Honoring the Past

Some schools and districts find they aren't immediately ready to jump into a visioning session. For some, it's because stakeholders feel they've "been there, done that;" for others, it's because bad feelings from past initiatives get in the way. Still others find that when they do try to move ahead and develop a new vision of what the school or district should be, longtime staff members resist, feeling that this quest dishonors or even dismisses their past contributions.

In this kind of situation, we recommend an activity we call the "Historygram" as a way to build a bridge between the past and the future and create a new values-driven vision that all can share. The Historygram process allows "tribal elders" (folks who have been around the longest of anyone in the organization) to talk about the values they have that have grown out of their experiences and to share information about past parades they joined or led (O'Neill, 2000b). It gives the entire school community the opportunity to reflect together in an effort to understand the patterns, cycles, and trends of their collective organizational history.

We begin the Historygram process by asking the assembled group to form a circle around the room's perimeter in the order they joined the school community,

| 2.5 | **A Sample Historygram Distribution** |

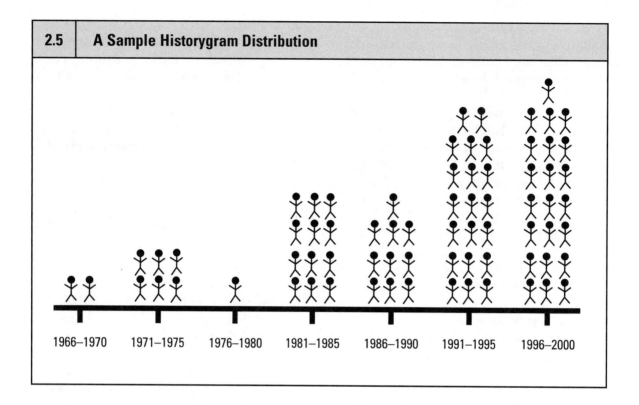

1966–1970 1971–1975 1976–1980 1981–1985 1986–1990 1991–1995 1996–2000

beginning with the "eldest tribal elder." We then divide the group into "eras," based on how many people came on board during different time periods of the school history. Next, we graph the results, as illustrated in Figure 2.5.

Each "era" group then develops a story-board showing the following information related to the time when they joined the school community:

- Major initiatives and goals.
- Major crises or turning points.
- Symbols, ceremonies, and traditions.
- What was happening in the world.
- What was happening in the community.
- A name or title for the era.
- Values they want to take into the future.

As each small group shares the story of its era, a designated historian captures this information on a collective poster (later to be used as the starting point for a visioning session). When all small groups have reported, the entire staff reassembles as a single large group to identify the themes, patterns, and cycles that have made up the school's history. Then they identify which patterns they want to continue and which they want to stop.

A Three-Step Process for Visioning

Once a school group is ready to develop a vision of the future, we often use a three-step process—brainstorming, creating affinity diagrams, and multi-voting—to help the staff identify elements of that preferred future and decide which ones are most compelling.

1. **Brainstorming.** When we introduce brainstorming, we remind the group that

quantity is more important than *quality*. Each person should let his or her mind roam free, not evaluating or discarding any ideas. We also provide plenty of time for silent reflection, and ask individuals to record their ideas on sticky notes, one idea per note.

2. **Creating Affinity Diagrams.** We invite the group members to place their sticky notes on a large poster board or wall space—still without talking—and group them by similarity or affinity. They can then begin talking about the ideas and naming the categories using header cards or larger sticky notes.

3. **Multi-voting.** Once the brainstormed ideas are grouped into categories based on similarity, we hand out sticky dots and ask everyone to cast votes for those categories they feel are most important to include in a vision statement. Each person gets a specific number of dots to attach to the sticky notes she or he feels best capture the vital elements of the vision.

This three-step visioning process will yield a limited number of ideas determined by the group to be the most important to include in the vision statement. Typically, groups delegate the actual writing of their vision statement to a subteam. The subteam shares its drafts with the larger group, and eventually, the process yields a version everyone agrees to support. This is the school's final vision statement.

Keeping a Vision Alive

Once created and captured in a formal statement, a vision will begin to "catch on" as people assimilate the vision statement's language and the thoughts and values it represents. One of the most powerful ways to move the vision statement out into the organization is to ask people what they think about it—whether they think the vision is feasible, something they could support, something they want and could commit to—and then listen respectfully, exploring what they have to say through dialogue. It is also important for leaders to *write* about what the vision means to them, sharing their reflections about the vision with the school community and inviting everyone's comments and suggestions for refining the statement.

It's through this sharing, and through ongoing modeling, reinforcement, and recognition, that a vision stays alive. Examples of how planners modeled and reinforced their visions abound in U.S. society. Martin Luther King Jr.'s "I Have a Dream" speech is a classic example of how one man's oft-repeated vision galvanized an entire movement. The suffragettes managed to gain voting rights for women because of their vision of having an equal voice in national politics. And hundreds of years after the writing of the Pledge of Allegiance—the embodiment of our forefathers' vision of "one nation, indivisible, with liberty and justice for all"—the words are still recited every day in classrooms and meeting halls throughout the United States. In each case, the originators of the vision were able to clearly and passionately articulate why their vision was such a compelling picture of a brighter future; in each case, people became part of the vision because they, too, began to believe in it.

You can reinforce a vision within your organization by continually encouraging people to dream and hope beyond the day; by using planning and goal-setting sessions that include visioning; and by providing time to pursue the vision and goals. When teachers or staff members are doing things that will lead to or enhance the vision, bringing those actions to the awareness of the individual and group helps them see how they contribute to the development of shared vision. These "visioning by grass fire" practices ultimately help people internalize the vision into their daily behavioral repertoire.

How will you know if your vision is alive and well in your school or district? The following criteria, adapted from Saphier and D'Auria (1993), provide guidance. You'll know a vision is alive when it

• *Permeates the institution*. It is embedded in contract language, communications, programs, and policies.

• *Drives all decisions*. It influences decisions related to budgeting, hiring, curriculum, assessment and instruction, union relations, and community partnerships.

• *Elicits strong reactions when it is violated*. Students, staff, families, and community members resist efforts to deviate from the vision's spirit and intent. Members of the school community who don't "fit" the vision often feel uncomfortable and may even choose to leave.

You can also detect vision at work by listening to the nature of daily conversations within school buildings. A great place to start is the faculty lounge. In *focused* schools, teachers informally share insights they've gained from reading professional literature, attending workshops and conferences, and observing their own students' responses to particular lessons, etc. The question that appears to underlie all these conversations is, "What do we need to change in our practices so we can reach all our students?" In *unfocused* schools, we've found that conversations tend to sound more like a running list of complaints— "problem kids," "pushy parents," "uncaring administration," "unfair mandates," and so on.

Establishing Strategic Priorities

All the elements of focus we've discussed—a common set of beliefs and core values, a clear and compelling mission statement, and a well-articulated vision—serve a number of functions within districts and schools. Obviously, they allow these organizations to set goals that will guide school and staff activity and effort. (See Chapter 5 for more about goals.) But another equally important function of these focus elements is their role in helping a school establish strategic priorities.

Consider the example of the Wisconsin Heights School District, a small, rural district where student athletics had long been a main priority. The district's budget reflected this value system; prior to 1998, Wisconsin Heights devoted more resources to improving athletic equipment and facilities than to staff development, curriculum development, and instructional programs combined.

Then in 1998, challenged and supported by renewed board leadership, a new superintendent, and the state and national focus on accountability, the district's educational community began a careful examination of their priorities. Using a highly inclusive process of visioning and needs assessment, Wisconsin Heights first realigned its core values and then revised its budget to reflect these values.

Today, a full-time director of curriculum and instruction leads the district's standards-based curriculum alignment, instruction, assessment, and staff development efforts. Individual schools plan their staff development around their student learning goals. The new Wisconsin Heights Educational Foundation, Inc., has established an expanded student scholarship fund. Both district and grant resources have been dedicated to developing partnerships with the community and the state as well as colleagues in institutions of higher education.

The realignment of activities and resources with the community's refreshed values and vision is resulting in strategic breakthroughs for the Wisconsin Heights School District. More students than ever before are involved in the district's "Rural Challenge" initiative focused on service learning, community building, and student empowerment in decision making. More families are being served through the district's Family Resource Center, which is reaching out to support, involve, and educate the families of all students. More teachers have clear professional goals and plans that are energizing them to learn more, try new approaches, and take more chances. Finally, test scores and other measures of student learning have improved in each of the three years since the district began its strategic planning process.

The Importance of Prioritizing

As the experience of Wisconsin Heights illustrates, developing strategic priorities means identifying what your school or district needs *to keep doing, stop doing,* and *start doing* in order to achieve your vision. It may require you to say no to projects that are appealing, but nonessential.

Of course, we have also worked with schools and districts that have identified more than 20 activities as "strategic priorities." This number is enough to tell us that these things are neither strategic nor really priorities. When an organization is acting strategically, it is *choosing* to do the things that will help achieve its vision of a better future, those things that reflect a deep

understanding of its current needs. The chosen activities and initiatives will create a bridge between identified needs and the challenges and opportunities that are on the horizon over the next five or more years.

When an organization has clear—and a manageable few—measurable priorities, those things will get done and the results will be evident to all. In contrast, when an organization has multiple unmeasurable priorities, there's lots of activity, but not much really gets done, and results are slow to come or nonexistent (see Sparks, 1999). Proper strategic prioritization is the difference between an improvement strategy that is "an inch deep and a mile wide" and one that is "an inch wide and a mile deep"— and gets below the surface to effect significant results and lasting change.

The Power of Pareto Thinking

"Pareto thinking" can help schools and districts to prioritize improvement strategies so that efforts are focused and aligned.

The Pareto principle was first defined by Vilfredo Pareto, a 19th century Italian economist. While studying the distribution of wealth, Pareto discovered that 80 percent of the wealth was held by 20 percent of the people. This basic finding has led to the practice of making financial and business decisions that target a small percentage of the population while influencing a large percentage of the wealth.

In the 1950s, Joseph Juran, a leading Quality Management thinker, author, and consultant, first applied the Pareto principle to management practices and came up with two simple tenets, which we have paraphrased below:

• Focus on improving the 20 percent *vital few* areas that will achieve the greatest gain and avoid the 80 percent *important many* areas that, although numerous in frequency, may provide less leverage.

• The *important many* areas are often related to the *vital few* areas. By focusing on improving the few, chances are you will address, solve, eliminate, or reduce the important many (Juran, 1995).

Pareto thinking is what led the Madison Metropolitan School District to reduce dozens of possible strategic priorities into just six. The district's 2005 Strategic Plan calls for (1) improved student achievement; (2) a safe, respectful learning environment; (3) a competent, diverse workforce; (4) strengthened partnerships; (5) a diverse, challenging curriculum; and (6) efficient use of resources. All initiatives, programs, and activities within the Madison Metropolitan School District are filtered through the lens of these strategic priorities. If something doesn't fit, it doesn't get the attention of the board and administration.

It appears the district's focus is beginning to pay dividends. In October 2000, local headlines trumpeted the news, "Black and Hispanic students narrow the gap" (Hall & Erickson, 2000). By going "an inch wide and a mile deep," the Madison Metropolitan School District is learning far more about what it takes to improve student achievement than they could possibly have learned if they tried to tackle every challenge at once.

We'll talk further about useful applications of the Pareto principle in Chapters 3 and 5.

Walking the Focus Talk

Building shared responsibility for student learning is a complex change process. Even if teachers and administrators have collaboration and teaming skills, have resources and support, and are implementing action plans, if they don't have a shared vision and a common focus, their efforts can only result in confusion (see Ambrose, 1987). The tendency to go our own way and do our own thing (so prevalent in education) takes over, and students experience learning as a series of unrelated individual units or blocks of time, with varying expectations, and little "glue" holding it all together. In such a system, students often fall through the cracks. Some do their "seat time" and graduate; others simply drop out.

In contrast, when teachers, staff and administrators are working in schools where *focus* is a part of everything they do, they have a deep sense of their collective "true north"—it helps them get unstuck when they don't know how to proceed and guides them back when they've lost their way. Students experience a rational and consistent system, one with a clear aim and consistent expectations. In such a system, all adults are deeply knowledgeable about the individual students, and there are fine-tuned processes for ensuring no student is left behind and all students are challenged.

Having a clear focus helps educational decision makers to say no. It enables schools to set priorities and reach consensus. Although all decisions may not necessarily reflect the option that will make everyone happy, decisions are always supported by fair and thoughtful reasoning.

Consider this example from Germantown Middle School. Staff and parents spent the better part of a year reaching agreement on the school's core values and vision, which they summarized as a statement of the school's philosophy. One year later, an upset coach stormed into the school's office. This coach was seeking the principal's intervention with an irate parent, who was angry because the girls' soccer team had been losing and his daughter—a star player—was getting no more playing time than any other player. The principal was understanding, but his response to the coach was firm:

> We spent the better part of last year developing a school philosophy statement with the input of hundreds of parents and staff. Nowhere in that statement will you see "winning" as one of our values. We want our kids to learn skills, to have fun, to enjoy being on a team together. These are core values of this school. You can share this philosophy statement with the parent and I'll back you up. If this experience isn't what that parent is looking for, perhaps the family might want to consider another school environment.

This was not the response the coach was looking for, but his reaction may surprise you: He relaxed and thanked the principal for reminding him of the firm ground beneath him. The next day, the coach had a long and productive conversation with the unhappy parent, and ultimately, the family chose to stay at Germantown Middle School.

M. Scott Peck (1987) believes that people yearn for community. "A real community,"

Peck says, "is, by definition immune to mob psychology because of its encouragement of individuality, its inclusion of a variety of points of view" (p. 64). And in schools, a loose group of people becomes a "community" when they have shared focus and shared responsibility. When we educators really listen to each other as we work to establish clear vision, mission, values, and priorities, we create school communities capable of meeting Peter Senge's challenge to sustain greatness.

Summary: Focus

Focus is a key element in the framework for building shared responsibility for student learning. Mendota Elementary School, Adlai Stevenson High School, Germantown Middle School, Madison Metropolitan School District, Verona Area School District, and many others are discovering the power they can unleash when they take the time to truly focus their work. These schools and districts are also finding that when they work on focus in the context of data, they enrich their perspective and create a synergistic energy that is greater than focus and data alone. In the next chapter, we'll examine the element of reflection and how it can be used to help keep the focus on student results.

3

Reflection

The real voyage in discovery consists not in seeking new landscapes
but in having new eyes.

—MARCEL PROUST

At last, with the referendum behind them and the brand new building
actually beginning to look like a middle school, Principal David Knoll*
can take a deep breath. Still, he knows the real work is yet to be done.
David is an experienced principal who has transferred to this district to take on
the challenge of building both a new facility and a new philosophy. He came
knowing that the atmosphere for change would be less than ideal, but that was
part of the allure for this steadfast advocate of learning.

Like so many districts across the nation, in recent years David's district has
been caught up in one political tug-of-war after another. Local radio talk show
hosts and media have fueled an intense debate challenging everything from the
district's curriculum and instruction to its strategic plan. Factions have formed
within the community, with parents and politicians demanding accountability.
Because the district has consistently produced test scores at or above the state
average, this public outcry seems unwarranted to many of the school staff and
administrators. Their general feeling is, "Perhaps if we keep a low profile, this
too shall pass."

If you look at what gets covered in this town's local media and in the larger
educational media, it's easy to see why these educators dismiss the testing and
accountability movement as another fad. So much of what has come and gone
in educational reform has had little lasting influence on the way schools operate. David's district has seen a parade of gurus pass by, each taking a turn in the
spotlight of reform. But despite tremendous initial fanfare, none of the heralded
improvement initiatives has brought about a fundamental change in these educators' daily lives. So why would the accountability movement, with all its

---

*David Knoll is a composite of principals we have worked with.

apparent political crudeness and flawed methodologies, be anything different?

As the saying goes, "People don't resist change, they resist *being changed*," (Scholtes, 1988, p. 1-21). To the eyes of many teachers and administrators in David's district, the accountability movement, as it is presently playing out, is an outsider's attempt to change the way in which education is delivered, monitored, and funded. David's challenge is to convince his staff that they really do need change—*change from within*. He must persuade them that this change, if embraced with an eye toward continuous improvement and learning, will usher in a new professionalism that will mean good things for children.

It's David's first day, and he is preparing for his initial meeting with a staff comprising both novice and experienced teachers. Some are voluntary transfers from other schools in the district and some have been hired in from other systems. As he prepares, David reflects on the sense of profound responsibility he feels for making this transition really matter. It's not just about moving into a new school, it's about an opportunity of a lifetime to make a difference in the lives of these teachers, these children, and these families.

Just before the meeting, as staff members begin to assemble, David reviews his notes one last time and then tosses them into a nearby trashcan. No, this one has to come from the heart. He welcomes his team and then begins to speak:

> Today marks the beginning of an exciting but difficult journey. All of us, including me, will be asked to examine some of our most deeply held beliefs about children, teaching, learning, and the professional role that each of us plays in ensuring that all of the children who attend this school

learn well. Together we will establish our mission, publicly articulate our core values, and create a vision for our new school. And, though I know this won't be popular, we will address the real and lasting concerns of our community by providing evidence that our students are learning. We will make a commitment to use data to inform our practice.

The room falls silent. Then, as murmurs began to swell into discourse, one of the veteran teachers raises his hand. "How are you going to assure us that this data won't be used against us?" he asks. Another teacher, who has been in the district for several years, adds, "We'll be crucified by the public and besides, we don't *have* any data except for the state test scores, and those are pretty darn good."

Feeling encouraged by the conversation's momentum, some of the newer teachers enter the debate. "Kids aren't measurable entities," one comments. "The most important things we do can't be measured," another adds. Then one brave teacher stands up to address the group:

> I've always been accountable for my students' progress. I'm the one who works with them every day. I'm the one who faces their parents at every reporting period. But that's not enough. This is obviously going to take time and learning on our part, but I don't think we have a choice anymore. To me, the most important thing is that we never reduce kids or our profession to numbers, but that we use whatever tools we can to make sure that what we're doing is really making a difference.

David breathes a sigh of relief. The journey has begun.

The brave teacher's perspective is characteristic of the highly competent educators we know. When you ask them why they chose education as a career, they'll tell you they were drawn to the profession by a strong sense of purpose and a profound commitment to children and learning. They believe in setting and maintaining high standards for all their students. What excites them most is the prospect of making young peoples' lives better through learning. They view their practice as the art of discovery through the dynamics of teaching and learning. Finally, they accept at a very deep level the responsibilities that come with their work.

And yet the myth persists that educators do not want to be held accountable. Perhaps the problem lies not in our commitment, or in our willingness to be accountable for what happens in the classroom, but in how we've come to define and implement accountability.

Data and Accountability

For many educators, "data" automatically conjures up two words and two words only: *test scores* and *accountability*. The association is unfortunate, because data should be more than test scores and are better used as learning tools than as a means for holding people accountable. As Figure 3.1 illustrates, educators have a choice about how we use data in our practice. Do we want to use it as an "extrinsic motivator" to reward or

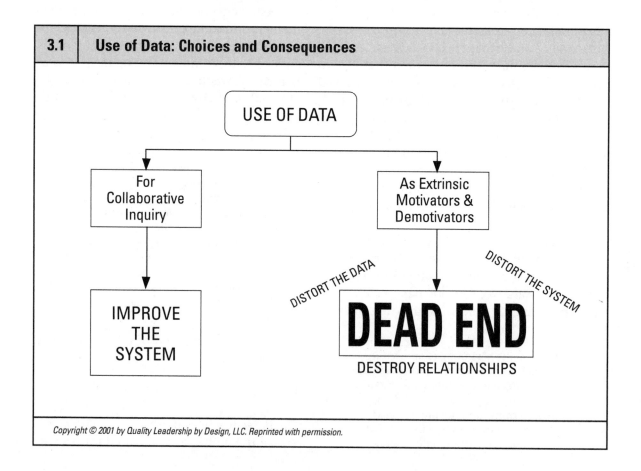

3.1	Use of Data: Choices and Consequences

punish people? Or do we want to use data as the basis for collaborative inquiry and learning that will help us discover better methods for doing our work?

The choice is an obvious one, probably because many educators have been past victims of "reward and punishment" data: *"Your test scores look great this year! Keep up the good work;" "Your test scores are lower this month than last month—what's going on?"* How much better to work in a system where data are used for inquiry: *"The scores look lower this month. Do we have enough data to tell if that's a trend? Are we doing something differently that is hindering our students' ability to learn well?"*

Three Ways to Improve Test Scores

We all want to improve test results for our students, our schools, and our districts. The question is, what do we need to *do* to get those improvements? When asked to show that our students' results are improving, we have three choices of response. We can (1) distort the test data to hide poor performance, (2) distort the system to provide different data outcomes, or (3) improve the system.

Choice #1: Distort test data to hide poor performance.

This is never an admirable choice, but it's certainly a natural and understandable one. It's particularly understandable in school systems where individual teachers and schools are under significant (but often subtle) pressure to demonstrate results, yet do not have access to the knowledge, tools, and methods that will allow them to achieve these results (O'Neill, 2001). "Distorting the data" is well illustrated by the true story of an administrator in Connecticut. Under pressure from the board to show

good test scores, he altered his school's test results for many years before he was finally caught. The school's curriculum, instruction, and programming hadn't changed—but the school's "results" certainly had.

Choice #2: Distort the system to provide different data outcomes.

Given the national attention on testing, "distorting the system" has become an unfortunately common occurrence. Schools and school systems drop whole segments of curriculum so that teachers may focus on preparing students to take standardized tests. Programs like art, music, and foreign language are scaled back in favor of a "focus on the basics."

How effective has this approach been? Two indicators of trouble: The gap between minority and nonminority achievement endures, and students in the United States continue to lag behind other countries in their math and science understanding (Gonzales et al., 2000).

Choice #3: Improve the system.

This third choice takes longer and is more arduous, but it leads to improved learning in the long run. It requires that people in the system understand that learning is actually a process of successive approximations.

Consider Tiger Woods for a moment: Was he always able to play golf with the skills that have brought him worldwide fame, or has he gotten better and better through discipline and practice? Is he accountable for his results because PGA Tour officials and his corporate sponsors "hold him to this," or because he feels a responsibility to his fans and to his own personal goals and has to demonstrate results in the process of playing the game? We suspect that the challenge of having to show what he can do is a more powerful determiner of increased motivation than even the millions of dollars Tiger earns in prize money and endorsements.

Likewise, teachers who share the results of their improvement efforts in an environment that supports and encourages "failing forward" as part of learning and improvement are placing themselves under as much performance pressure as any reward/punishment policy can create. A commitment to *improving the system* is the guiding force for building shared responsibility for student learning.

Data Are Inescapable

Educators' ultimate ability to redefine the use of standardized tests (and the accompanying carrot-and-stick approach to accountability) will depend largely on our willingness to embrace data as tools for learning. One thing is clear: In the absence of any alternative definition of accountability, the present scenario—which emphasizes reward and punishment—will prevail. What the courageous teacher in David's school knows is that policymakers and the general public are not likely to return to the day where hunches and feelings drove decisions. In this century, the use of data will drive technological, economic, and social change.

One reason to suspect that the United States' infatuation with the use of data in policymaking is likely to continue is because there's something very "American" about it. We love to measure, count, and number everything. Consider this anecdote shared by Anne Meek, our editor, about her evening at a Braves–Mets game in Atlanta's Turner Stadium:

> Every time a batter walked up to home plate, his stats were shown on a huge digital screen, and the results of his turns at bat during this game were also shown. Every time the pitcher threw a ball,

another screen told us the miles per hour number of that pitch. On another screen, the progress of the other American League games was charted, with the players' numbers and their stats. The program even gives the players' birthdays! The ballgame makes me think that educators don't have it so bad. At least when we stand up, there is no screen telling the public how many times we've struck out or what our batting averages are! And we don't have our birthdays printed in the paper.

Whether or not we'd like to admit it, there is a competitive mentality that permeates our culture. Simply put, keeping score is as American as apple pie . . . or baseball.

But look closer and you'll see why the use of data for school improvement—and not just school accountability—isn't just a passing fad; the fact is it works. In 1998, the U.S. Department of Education published a report titled *Turning Around Low-Performing Schools* that made a strong case for the use of data to support problem solving in schools struggling with low performance. The report states, "Measuring progress and setting standards and analyzing the information to identify patterns of failure and their causes enables schools and districts to diagnose low performance and attack specific problems with concrete solutions" (Doherty & Abernathy, 1998, p. 30).

Lowell School is a good example. An urban elementary school that has consistently posted improved student results over the past three years, Lowell sets aside nine days each year to support classroom teachers' efforts to individually assess their students, collaboratively analyze their assessment results, and determine flexible groupings and approaches based on those results. Together, Lowell staff and their principal, Sue Abplanalp, view this commitment to schoolwide reflection as a continuous, never-ending process. This year, the faculty has decided to target the specific skill sets and needs of special education students to prepare these children to take part in the state testing program.

Admittedly, using data as problem-solving tools to improve low performing schools is important, but using data for reflective learning isn't just for the purpose of "fixing what's wrong." In a world where change is a constant, all schools are faced with the need to continuously monitor and improve their performance. Using data for both planning and implementation is a common theme in accounts of successful school improvement efforts (see Educational Research Service, 1999).

A Process for Schoolwide and Systemwide Learning

This chapter presents a sampling of success stories where school improvement efforts

based on an understanding of data are working. We want to emphasize that the educators we focus on use data as a *learning tool,* not as an incentive or a disincentive for change. We believe that data, like a mirror, gives educators feedback about our systems, our students, and ourselves. That is why we refer to the use of data for improvement as *reflection.*

The process of reflection allows educators to test our assumptions, validate our logic, and research the efficacy of our actions. As illustrated in Figure 3.2, the process begins with an important question or a need to know. Logic leads to an investigation of the data, which in turn, leads to another set of logical questions.

To illustrate this process, let's visit an elementary school that applied the reflective process to its students' results on the state's 3rd grade reading exam. Staff began with this important question: "How did our students do on this year's exam?" Logic led

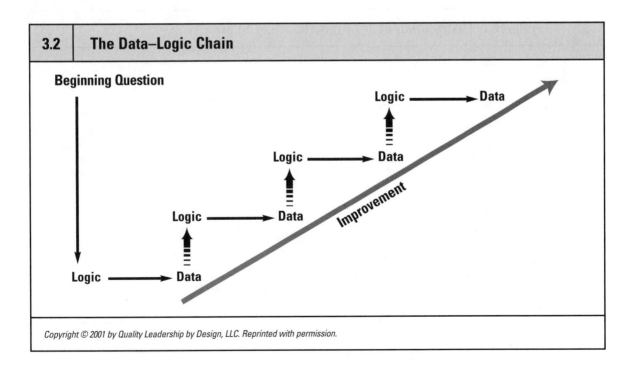

3.2 | **The Data–Logic Chain**

Beginning Question

Logic ——→ Data

Logic ——→ Data

Logic ——→ Data

Logic ——→ Data

Improvement

them to look at the data—their school's average score—which was 48.5 out of a possible 60 points. Considering that the state had established a score of 33 as "meeting the standard," this school's average score looked pretty good.

From this data, the teachers proceeded to their next question: "How did our students do compared to the other elementary schools in our district?" Again, logic led them to examine the data—the average scores for the district's two other elementary schools, which were 52.2 and 49.8. Suddenly, their school's average score of 48.5 no longer looked quite so good.

Again, the data cycled the teachers back into logical inquiry. They decided to look deeper into their own data for the answer to this question: "How many of our students met or exceeded the standard of 33 out of 60?" The frequency diagram in Figure 3.3 shows the number of reading test items this school's 3rd graders answered correctly (individual student scores) and the number of students receiving those scores.

As you see, the range of student test performance was vast—from a low score of 19 to a high score of 60. Also, there appeared to be two different *sets* of scores, as evidenced by the two peaks on the chart. (Statisticians call this a bimodal distribution.) One set of scores clustered around a mode of 42; a second set clustered around a mode of 56.

This data pattern sparked lively staff discussion about what might be occurring within the school to produce such results. How could children all attending the same school have such different outcomes? Questioning then focused on the children whose scores were represented as tailing off the lower ends of the chart—those students

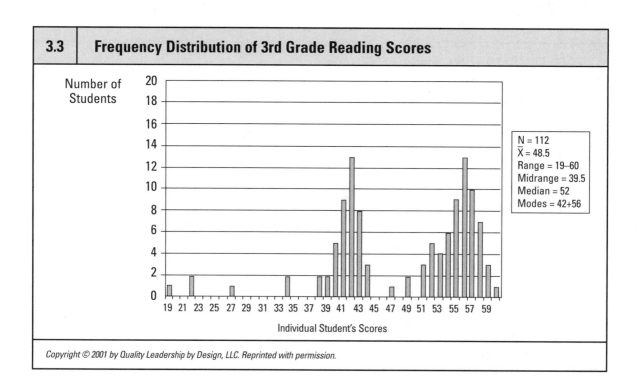

| 3.3 | **Frequency Distribution of 3rd Grade Reading Scores** |

N = 112
X̄ = 48.5
Range = 19–60
Midrange = 39.5
Median = 52
Modes = 42+56

Individual Student's Scores

who were definitely not meeting the standard. Finally, logic led the teachers to ask, "If this score distribution pattern is true for *this* group—our 3rd grade reading students—might it also be true for our students in the other grade levels?"

The next step in the data–logic chain was clear: The staff needed to know more about their lowest functioning students so that they could determine which factors might be differentiating the performance of these children from the performance of their peers. Teachers identified their four lowest-performing students; then the entire staff brainstormed what they wanted to know about these children. Here is their list of questions:

- Who are they?
- Where do they live?
- What are their strengths? Weaknesses? Skill gaps?
- What is their attendance?
- Did they begin school at earlier age than most of their peers?
- Are they new to the district? New to the school?
- Are there any gender or race patterns among these students?
- Do their parents attend conferences?
- What is their family configuration?
- Have they been referred for behavioral reasons?
- Do they attend and use the reading and math centers?

School secretaries contributed to the reflective process by assembling a data profile on the targeted group of students and creating bar charts to display the numbers. The results were surprising and countered a number of preconceived notions. For example, teachers assumed they would find that the parents of the lowest-achieving children did not attend teacher conferences; in fact, the data showed these parents attended

conferences regularly, even more so as the children got older. It also turned out that lowest-achieving children were *not* relatively young compared to their classmates. Furthermore, there were no noticeable gender or race patterns. What the teachers did discover was that *mobility* and *attendance* were two factors that differentiated the lowest-achieving students from their peers.

Commenting on these findings, the school principal said:

> I knew that the teachers knew intuitively who their struggling children were, but they didn't know what all the struggling students might have in common—information that would give us some answers about what we as a school community could do to help the struggling students. Once mobility and attendance were identified as issues for most of these students, the conversations became much richer. Teachers began to reflect together on what it must feel like to be a child who comes and goes from our school. They asked, "How can we be better at helping them deal with their feelings of loss, fear, apathy and inadequacy?" "Would I continue to attend if these were my circumstances?" "What kind of system do we need to create to make sure their academic growth is effected as positively as possible when they are with us?" "What can we do to encourage their attendance?"

The process of schoolwide reflection has led this school down a path very different from the one it would have traveled if staff had been content to simply know that their 3rd graders did "pretty well" on the state test. Figure 3.4 provides a recap of this school's data–logic chain. What began as a series of questions about test performance and a set of assumptions about children who struggle in school ultimately yielded a set of solutions aimed at school and system improvements that would support student success.

3.4 | Elementary School's Data–Logic Chain

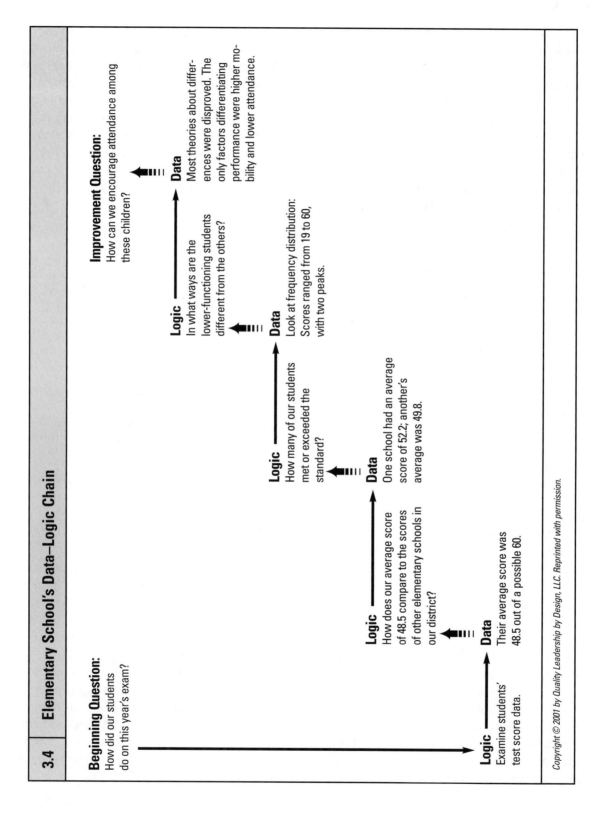

Beginning Question:
How did our students do on this year's exam?

Logic ⟶
Examine students' test score data.

Data
Their average score was 48.5 out of a possible 60.

Logic ⟶
How does our average score of 48.5 compare to the scores of other elementary schools in our district?

Data
One school had an average score of 52.2; another's average was 49.8.

Logic ⟶
How many of our students met or exceeded the standard?

Data
Look at frequency distribution: Scores ranged from 19 to 60, with two peaks.

Logic ⟶
In what ways are the lower-functioning students different from the others?

Data
Most theories about differences were disproved. The only factors differentiating performance were higher mobility and lower attendance.

Improvement Question:
How can we encourage attendance among these children?

A Tool for Personal Learning

Meet Virginia Kester. Ginny is a high school teacher in an urban district who designs and teaches a skills-based elective class to help 9th grade students improve their reading, writing, organization, and study skills. Most of Ginny's students are at the 5th stanine or lower in reading and writing as measured by the state standardized tests they took as 8th graders.

Ginny works closely with her students and their families to create, communicate, and monitor learning goals for the whole class and for each student. She administers a series of homemade classroom assessments throughout the year and charts student progress. In June, she examines each student's individual progress as measured by these classroom assessments and uses the students' grade point averages and their state test results to assess the effectiveness of her instructional program. Based on data Ginny collects, she makes adjustments to her program and continuously improves her teaching strategies from year to year.

Ginny Kester is a master of *reflection*, constantly asking, "How are my students doing?" and constantly using multiple sources of data to study and enhance her teaching practice. Ginny's classes provide living proof that reflection contributes to improved achievement. Of the 40 students enrolled in her classes over the last two years, 73 percent improved at least one stanine in writing; 48 percent improved one stanine or more in reading. When Ginny disaggregated this data, she discovered her African American students had made especially encouraging progress: 75 percent improved at least one stanine in writing and 50 percent improved two stanines or more; 58 percent improved one or more stanines in reading.

Tapping Multiple Sources of Information

Let's take a closer look at the various kinds of data Ginny Kester uses to inform reflection and improve her practice.

Quantitative data.
This information lets Ginny know if her instructional approach has produced the hoped-for outcomes. *Standardized test scores* provide her with an initial starting point for learning about her students. These data are available, relatively easy to interpret, and provide an adequate baseline for determining the general need for her services. In addition, she uses custom-designed *classroom assessments* to measure student progress throughout the course of instruction. These two quantitative data sources serve different purposes, and in combination, they give Ginny an ongoing, quantitative picture of her students' progress.

Qualitative data.
Ginny also relies on qualitative information she gleans from student records and from conversations with her peers, the students, and their parents. Qualitative data can be acquired through a variety of methods including observation, surveys and questionnaires, interviews, and focus groups. This kind of data enhances a purely quantitative approach by helping teachers learn more about the specific elements of the teaching process that parents or students find useful. In Ginny's case, qualitative data gives her a more complete picture of how each group perceives and reacts to a particular program or instructional strategy.

Intuitive data.

Finally, Ginny uses her professional expertise and "teacher's intuition" to gain a deeper understanding of her students' needs—an understanding beyond what any test score could tell her. Many teachers claim they know their students have learned because they "can see it in their eyes." Well, that's true to a great extent. Using one's intuition falls into the realm of the *art* of teaching. Intuition is a legitimate and important source of information for teachers, but it can take many years of practice to develop these powers of perception. Thus, as a reflective tool, intuition provides experienced professionals additional information about their students' learning.

Skillful teachers know how to balance the science and the art of their teaching. On one hand we need to ask, "How can we use numerical and descriptive data (the science) to validate what our intuition and professional knowledge and experience tell us?" But we also need to ask, "How can we bring our professional knowledge and wisdom (our art) to the process in a way that helps us understand and critically question the data?" This interplay between the science and art of teaching is what elevates compassion to professionalism.

In this way, both qualitative and intuitive data can illuminate the meaning of quantitative data. In Ginny's case, her students' standardized test results may not match what she knows her students' capabilities to be, based on their classroom performance on tasks or assessments that measure similar skills or knowledge. In such situations, Ginny would use intuitive knowledge to inform her inquiry into the quantitative data her students have produced. She might also survey her colleagues' perceptions of her students'

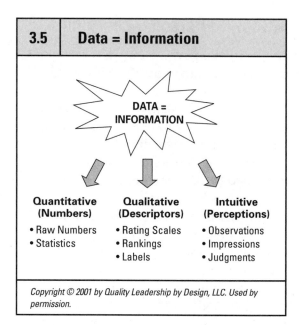

| 3.5 | Data = Information |

DATA = INFORMATION

Quantitative (Numbers)
- Raw Numbers
- Statistics

Qualitative (Descriptors)
- Rating Scales
- Rankings
- Labels

Intuitive (Perceptions)
- Observations
- Impressions
- Judgments

capabilities, thus tapping one of many sources of qualitative information.

The theme here is that data provide us with *information,* nothing more and nothing less. As Figure 3.5 illustrates, this information may be in the form of numbers, descriptors, or perceptions. The more sources of information we seek out, the more well-rounded our understanding of any situation will be.

Using Feedback to Promote Professional Efficacy

When applied with knowledge and integrity, data heighten our ability to make informed and reasoned decisions about our work; this kind of reflection is what distinguishes the professional practitioner from the technician. In medicine, the law, athletics, and the arts, shared learning, research, public scrutiny, feedback on performance, and peer review are standard professional practice. Why wouldn't we expect the same level of professional rigor from our teachers? Education is not just about methods and textbooks; it's about being able to demonstrate through the student performance that the instruction provided has resulted in learning.

Ginny Kester finds data to be an essential element of her reflective practice and her own professionalism. Her peers describe her as a "master teacher," and in conversations with Ginny, her sense of personal efficacy as a professional is obvious. Teachers' sense of efficacy is tightly linked with a high degree of professional engagement. Tschannen-Moran and colleagues (1998) note, "The perception that a performance has been successful affects the effort [teachers] put into teaching, the goals they set, and their level of aspiration" (p. 222).

In our own work, we have often noticed that reflective practice provides teachers a powerful and much needed feedback mechanism that further enhances their feelings of efficacy. Teachers feel a profound sense of accomplishment when they *know* their instructional efforts have translated into learning. Cathy Hunt, a kindergarten teacher at Mendota Elementary School, said it best: "Feedback keeps me going. It keeps me wanting to learn more, wanting to expand, wanting to see what else I can do. It makes my expectations for myself higher. I tend to work a lot harder if I'm getting feedback."

At the individual level, reflection on student performance data provides teachers with valuable feedback about the nature and the extent of the impact they are having on their students. They know that what they are doing is making a difference. Without the feedback data provide, teachers can only guess (and hope) that their students have achieved the desired outcomes. Again,

Cathy Hunt shares why data are so important to her:

> I find using data reinforcing. It's more reinforcing to me to be able to see this is what [students] did instead of just having a gut feeling. A gut feeling doesn't always feel good and it doesn't prove anything. I could say, "Yes, he knows how to read," but if he can't read for the next person, it's not saying much, and I'm not going to get the feedback I need, either.

Using Feedback to Promote Student Responsibility for Learning

The data that Ginny uses in her classroom are called "snapshot" pictures because they tell her how her students are performing *at a given moment in time* on a particular measure. Snapshot pictures are good for comparing how different, distinct groups of students are doing relative to each other. They are also useful for comparing pre- and post-assessment results for any individual student or subgroup of students.

But snapshots have their limitations. Educators should also develop "moving pictures" of our students' performance by comparing the same measures over time. Figure 3.6 contrasts these two techniques for getting performance feedback and shows how each might be used to monitor ongoing quantitative, qualitative, and intuitive data.

Moving pictures fill out the performance story by capturing information that snapshots cannot. They let us track student performance over time, identify trends and patterns, and verify whether true sustained progress has been made. In the classroom, providing ongoing feedback to students about their progress helps motivate them to take ownership of their learning. Here's an illustration of how teachers might use

3.6	Snapshots and Moving Pictures		
Type of Data	**Quantitative Examples**	**Qualitative Examples**	**Intuitive Examples**

Snapshot
 	
Individual data point
—a moment in time
	• One year's test results
	• Attendance on a
	  single day
		• Reponses to a
		  single survey
		• Information from a
		  focus group
			• A single observation

Moving Picture
 	
Many data points
over time
	• Many years of test
	  data (same test)
	• Attendance over time
		• Log of behavioral
		  referrals for a
		  semester
		• Responses to
		  repeated surveys
			• An impression based
			  on years of experience

continuous progress data in the classroom as a way to engage and motivate students.

Shannon Greaves is a middle school language arts teacher in a mid-sized suburban school district. Without any specific training in how to use data for instructional improvement, Shannon simply did what came naturally. She began by creating and posting a simple chart showing her 6th graders' average score on their weekly spelling test. Every Monday, she would record the results of the previous week's test, creating what statisticians call a "run chart." Figure 3.7 shows the first 11 weeks of Shannon's chart.

Before long, Shannon noticed that her data-gathering activities were spurring student interest in their spelling test performance. They could hardly wait to see their scores each week. Shannon also noticed that there seemed to be a direct correlation between the test results and her students' moods. Were the results influencing the mood swings or was it the other way

3.7	Run Chart of Spelling Test Results: 1st Quarter

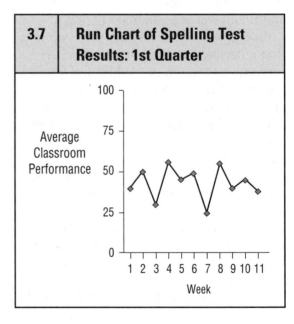

around? With 6th graders, it was difficult to know for sure.

By the end of the first quarter—a total of 11 weeks—the spelling test run chart was beginning to reveal a dramatic variation in performance from one week to the next. Surmising that there was more to this phenomenon than hormones could explain,

Shannon decided to inquire into the reasons for the students' sporadic performance. And true to her student-centric style, she chose to engage her class in data analysis. "What do you think is causing our chart to go up and down so much?" Shannon asked her students.

The students had a number of hypotheses, and they brainstormed ways they might be able to perform more consistently on the weekly spelling test and improve the overall class performance. They came up with some strategies they could use themselves, such as "studying the words every night and without the television on to distract us." They also pointed out a few things they thought Shannon could do to help boost scores ("Use fun games and activities to practice the words") and some things their parents could do ("Help us go over the words each night"). Shannon, the parents, and the students all agreed to try these strategies during the second quarter.

As the next 11 weeks passed, Shannon kept plotting the scores of the weekly spelling test. The results, shown in Figure 3.8, were dramatic in two ways: Not only did the class performance improve markedly during the second quarter, the scores were much more consistent.

During the first 11 weeks, students' scores bounced around a lot, varying as much as 15 or more points from one week to the next. Just by eyeballing Figure 3.8, you can see that the overall weekly average hovered around 40 points. During the second 11-week quarter, *after* the students had discussed their results and the class began making changes in the way they approached the teaching and learning of spelling words, there was much less variation in performance from week to week. Scores clustered tightly around 75 points. We suspect spelling test scores in Shannon's class continued to improve as the year went on.

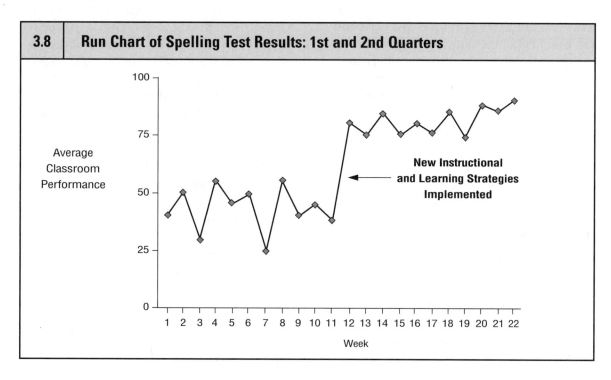

3.8 **Run Chart of Spelling Test Results: 1st and 2nd Quarters**

Average Classroom Performance

New Instructional and Learning Strategies Implemented

Week

✧ ✧ ✧ ✧ ✧

Teachers like Shannon Greaves and Ginny Kester intuitively know that the power of data resides in how we use it for continuous learning and improvement. This power increases exponentially when data are regularly monitored and analyzed in collaboration with students, other teachers, administrators, and parents on an ongoing basis.

Research validates this intuition. Several recent studies have shown that students' active engagement in their own learning—including the assessments of this learning—makes a positive and substantial difference in terms of their achievement (see Newmann, Secada & Wehlage, 1995). Student engagement in the form of individual and collective reflection is a powerful way to motivate young people to take charge of their learning. This is a basic premise of shared responsibility.

Teachers can help increase the effort students invest in learning by providing them with good tools for reflection as a class and as individuals. Portfolios, journals, charts and graphs, rubrics, and peer feedback are all useful tools for engaging students in individual self-reflection. Keeping classroom data available to students in the form of easy-to-understand, visual displays can have tremendous impact on the group as a whole. Once Shannon's class could *see* their spelling test results, the entire class felt responsible for *improving* the results.

A Tool for Professional Development

In Muskego-Norway, a suburban school district just outside Milwaukee, teachers and administrators engage in reflection on an ongoing basis. What began as a graduate school assignment for Jo Ellen Pirlott,

Muskego-Norway's reading coordinator and staff developer, kicked off a new way of doing business throughout the district.

When Jo Ellen asked for teacher volunteers to engage in a classroom action research project to collaboratively study the district's reading strategies' effect on student achievement, a team of 3rd grade teachers from Tess Corners Elementary School stepped up to the task.

In the action research project, the Tess Corners team assessed their students' reading proficiencies against districtwide standards and benchmarks. The assessment strategy included four performance assessments conducted over four months, with specific interventions applied consistently in the classrooms of all research team members. Each student read the same four passages; teachers measured progress according to the same rubric.

Over the course of the project, the Tess Corners team examined the data they were gathering on their students' specific reading strengths and weaknesses. They expanded this review process into meaningful discussions about what each team member was doing or *not* doing in each of the identified skill areas. What methods, for example, were individual teachers using to teach students how to make inferences and draw conclusions?

The Tess Corners team learned a lot from these discussions. For one thing, they learned there was very little consistency in their individual approaches in terms of content and the amount of time they devoted to reading instruction. They found that certain skills weren't being taught at all. For example, no one was teaching students to be good test-takers, a valuable skill that could help students better demonstrate their learning. The team also learned that they had set their initial performance goals too low; by their own standards, they were able to meet these goals too easily. Finally, these teachers learned there were certain things that they simply had to *stop doing* in order to get better results. Teacher Micki Daily put it this way: "We had too much on our raft. We had to decide what to toss off the boat. We needed more focused time to teach the skills that our students were lacking."

Enlightened and empowered by these insights, the Tess Corners team began to adjust their instructional approaches—and they quickly saw very gratifying improvements in student performance. As Figure 3.9 shows, in November, at the start of the initiative, 55.6 percent of Tess Corners 3rd graders scored at the proficient or advanced level; by February, that number had increased to 80 percent.

The data-based reflection that began as part of a four-month research project is now standard practice at Tess Corners. The teachers will admit that sometimes "it's a

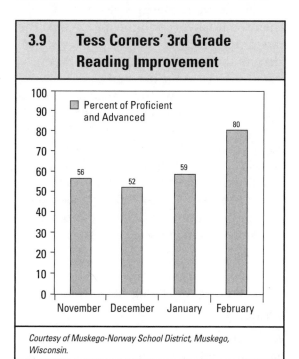

3.9	Tess Corners' 3rd Grade Reading Improvement

Courtesy of Muskego-Norway School District, Muskego, Wisconsin.

pain in the neck to collect the data," but all agree that it helps them know their students better. They also comment that the team approach to data gathering and reflection is tremendously valuable and claim that mutual support and collegial problem solving really help maintain their ongoing efforts on behalf of students. As teacher Janis Schwalbach notes, "We collectively buy into this. It's naturally aligned with how we think and what we believe." Another teacher, Jane Plemons, adds, "We've gotten really specific in our interventions. We can see the gains in reading."

Teachers at Tess Corners Elementary, and other teachers described in this chapter, have all begun to see that working together on reflection addresses some of the fundamental teaching issues they've had for years. According to Tess Corners Principal Jo Ann Kehl:

> This process translates into self-inflicted rigor. When teachers in our building shared what they were learning, it raised questions about what they were teaching and about what was being taught in other classrooms and in previous grades. Teachers know their colleagues are depending on them. Accountability crosses the grade levels, and teachers are talking about learning everywhere. That's an indicator to me that this is becoming internalized.

A Collaborative Learning Process

The next chapter provides an in-depth discussion of *collaboration,* the third support of our framework for shared responsibility. But it's impossible to discuss reflection without also discussing the need for people to work collectively to broaden organizational learning. Collaborative reflection can occur within departments, cross-curricular teams, and grade-level teams (like at Tess Corners) or throughout an entire school. Regardless of the group's configuration, reflecting together builds organizational capacity for learning.

One useful way to engage groups in collaborative reflection is to conduct a needs assessment that includes a cross-section of stakeholders in the community. This can be done as a school or as a district. We have found that at all organization levels, using a variety of data-gathering techniques aimed at assessing a variety of needs helps to target improvement efforts and provides important baseline information for monitoring progress. The needs assessment process typically includes the examination of both quantitative and qualitative data about

- Student achievement.
- Order, discipline, and school climate.
- Parent and community involvement.
- Staff, student, parent, and community satisfaction.
- Curriculum and instruction.
- Postgraduate success.

The needs assessment process works best as a collaborative effort, with groups of staff, parents, and community members working together to design and implement their needs assessment strategies. The dialogue can reveal the assumptions, perceptions, and beliefs that stakeholders bring to the table. This group-exchange also provides a perfect venue for collaborative reflection; first, as a way to explore differences in perceptions and second, as a way to inquire into the data to check the accuracy of those perceptions.

There are many ways to gather data in a needs assessment process. A few of the better-known methods are surveys, questionnaires, and interviews, all of which require a certain level of expertise in terms of question development, sampling, distribution, and analysis. Some districts ask personnel with marketing or research expertise to take charge of developing data-gathering

instruments; others hire expertise on a contracted basis or purchase off-the-shelf products. The important thing is for the data-gathering process to be as scientifically rigorous as possible, so that it will yield valid and reliable information.

Of course, there are other data-gathering techniques that provide excellent information without requiring the same level of methodological rigor. For example, teachers, parents, and students have a tremendous amount of untapped perspective about what needs "fixing" within the learning environment. One school we worked with tapped into this resource by conducting brainstorming sessions with staff, parent, and community groups to identify the critical issues facing the school. They came up with 27 issues. Next, staff, parents, and community stakeholders examined these issues and used a multi-vote process (five votes per person, to be spent on one issue or distributed among several) to reduce the 27 issues to more manageable number. Then the teachers and principal applied the Pareto principle (see Chapter 2, page 33) to identify the *vital few* critical issues they would subject to further study.

Figure 3.10 shows the five issues this particular school ultimately identified as the areas it most needed to address in order to improve student achievement. Small teams of teachers and other school staff went on to study the top five categories to determine the extent to which these issues were truly problematic and to identify deeper and more specific reasons why the issues existed.

The Next Step in Needs Assessment: Method 1

Where does your school go once you have narrowed down the problematic issues to a manageable number? Here's how a

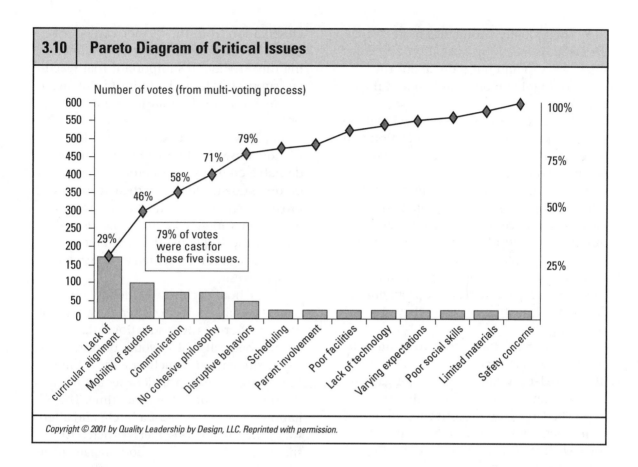

3.10 | Pareto Diagram of Critical Issues

Number of votes (from multi-voting process)

29%
46%
58%
71%
79%

79% of votes were cast for these five issues.

100%
75%
50%
25%

Lack of curricular alignment
Mobility of students
Communication
No cohesive philosophy
Disruptive behaviors
Scheduling
Parent involvement
Poor facilities
Lack of technology
Varying expectations
Poor social skills
Limited materials
Safety concerns

faculty meeting might unfold in a real school setting.

1. The meeting begins on a positive note, with a quick check-in designed to get the group focused on students. Tonight, the meeting facilitator uses the "light bulb" check-in: "When during this past week did you see the light bulb go on for a student in your class? Describe the student's reaction." To ensure the entire meeting isn't spent exchanging stories, this activity is limited to 10 minutes.

2. The group reviews the agenda. The plan is to meet this afternoon for 45 minutes. There are two activities to complete. After confirming there are no last-minute items to add to the agenda, they launch into the first activity.

3. The large group breaks into five smaller groups, each focused on one of the top five critical issues listed on the Pareto chart: curriculum, mobility, communications, philosophy, and discipline. (The groups could be formed randomly or on a volunteer basis according to individual interest. The only "rule" is that every teacher must participate in a study group. If possible, achieving grade-level or departmental diversity within the groups is desirable.)

4. For the next 20 minutes, the small groups generate questions around their issues:

• The Curriculum Group wants to know what already exists that might be considered best practice in each of the content areas.

• The Mobility Group digs more deeply into what is meant by "mobility" and considers ways to find out more about the needs of highly mobile children and their families.

• The Communications Group identifies some of the barriers to communication and develops a set of questions to pursue with parents and other staff members.

• The Philosophy Group mulls over the school's mission and values statements to look for guidance on how each statement might apply to students with special needs.

• The Discipline Group generates a list of data sources that might provide more information on specific types of problematic behaviors and when or where they are occurring.

5. Each small group uses two minutes to summarize its results for the rest of the faculty and identify the next steps for gathering additional information on its issue.

6. The large group reconvenes for a brief wrap up and sets the agenda for the following week's faculty meeting. The meeting concludes on time.

Although this method of data gathering is not highly scientific in terms of its statistical validity, it effectively uses quantitative, qualitative, and intuitive data and statistically sound principles to achieve focus and clarity. We recommend it as a time-efficient way to involve large numbers of people in determining and understanding school needs.

The Next Step in Needs Assessment: Method 2

Another useful approach to getting feedback about your teaching and learning system is through the use of "friendly observers," who visit the school and its classrooms and give a report on what they see.

Observation from the outside can be perceived as threatening, so prior to launching this method, it's important that teachers, support staff, and administration agree on the ground rules that will guide the process.

In one school, the staff selected its friendly observers by first brainstorming desirable criteria such as professional expertise, knowledge in a particular subject or program, reputation, and trustworthiness. Next, they generated a list of names and selected the 10 people they felt best met the criteria and represented a diverse set of perspectives.

This school decided the friendly observers should be free to enter classrooms at any time during the instructional day—unless teachers felt that it would be disruptive to the students, in which case they simply hung a sign outside the door requesting that the observer return at another time. The visitations went off without a hitch, and afterward, the friendly observers gathered to share what they had seen and prepare a collaborative report to the school staff highlighting areas of need. This information, along with a thorough study of the curriculum, a review of student achievement data, and data from a staff survey, served as the basis for the school's improvement goals.

A Means for Assessing System Performance

"Area High School in Trouble!" Almost all of us are familiar with this type of newspaper headline and with a story that usually accompanies it: a challenge to the board of education to explain why the ACT or SAT scores of graduates from this school are always so much lower than scores from a neighboring school. Typically, the story will also provide test scores from the last two years or so and suggest that Area High's performance is dropping while that of the nearby high school is stable.

When faced with this kind of public thrashing, a school board's typical reaction is to find someone to blame. A board that understands the power of reflection as a means for assessing system performance would take a much different approach. It would look for data that could help clarify the performance capability of the two high schools being compared.

The first step would be to look at the basic facts. Let's say that in 1999, the average ACT score at Area High was a full point below its average score for 1998 and a point-and-a-half below its average score for 1997. Looks like a downward trend, doesn't it?

Fortunately, the school board in our example also knows that two or even three moments in a "moving picture" of school performance do not provide enough data to determine whether an apparent trend is real or not. The board decides to go all the way back to 1990 and plot Area High's average ACT scores over 10 years. Figure 3.11 shows the results. What does this data reveal about the school's performance? Was the newspaper headline accurate? Is "Area High School in Trouble"?

Understanding Data Variation

All too often, newspapers' reactions to school test scores demonstrate an incomplete understanding of the data and, more importantly, of data *variation*. Variation in test scores—the amount and pattern of "ups and downs" the data show—is as natural as variation in the amount of time it might take you to get to work from one day to the next.

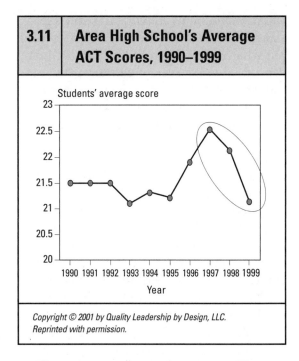

| 3.11 | Area High School's Average ACT Scores, 1990–1999 |

There are two types of variation. The first, *special cause variation,* is created by a specific situation, circumstance, or anomaly. An example might be a traffic accident that causes a back up of many miles and adds an hour to your commute—or, in the case of test scores, a fire drill during test administration that causes students to lose focus. The second type of variation, *common cause variation,* is created by factors that are present all the time—that are inherent in how the system was designed—but add up differently each day, week, or year. Examples of common cause variation in our traveling-to-work example include how far you live from your workplace and the highway design that forces six lanes of traffic to merge into four one mile before your exit. In education, common cause variation might be due to factors such as curriculum, school board and administrative policies, and budget allocations.

The course of action necessary to reduce data variation depends on what type of variation you're faced with. To reduce special cause variation, you would need to find out what was different in that specific incident, then either seek to eliminate the cause of a problem (or, if the unexpected outcome is a desirable one, to replicate the situation). In contrast, the only way to reduce common cause variation is to look at *all the data* and make a *fundamental change* to the system in a way that would affect all the factors present.

Determining the type of variation test scores illustrate is only possible when you examine data over time. You must have more than two or three data points before you can know whether the ups and downs in any given pattern reflect common or special cause variation.

Look again at Figure 3.11. What kind of variation is going on at Area High? What appears to be a downward trend from 1997–1999 may in fact be a return to what the system is really capable of producing. In other words, the higher average scores in 1997 and 1998 could be due to special causes; 1999's lower scores could reflect what's normal for Area High. If what we're seeing really *is* special cause variation, the appropriate improvement strategy would be different from the tact to take if the school is experiencing a true downward trend. But at this point, with only this data available, we can't tell whether any of these score changes are statistically significant.

Factoring Variation into Reflection

Unfortunately, more often than not, school district leaders react to common cause variation with special cause solutions, and in doing so, throw the system into even greater variation and lack of predictability. (This is referred to as "tampering.") District leaders who understand common and

special cause variation can use data to determine what the system is likely to produce, given its present design and management strategy. If those results are satisfactory, a continuous improvement strategy will produce ever-improving results. If they are unsatisfactory, a fundamental systematic change will be required to achieve better results.

Let's return to the newspaper article about Area High. It mentioned two concerns: the apparent downward trend in test scores at Area High and the school's relatively poor performance when compared with a neighboring high school. We've already examined the first concern, and we have determined we need more information before we can know whether a trend is occurring (and subsequently, decide the best course of action).

The second concern is more complex than a quick look at the numbers would suggest. To begin with, because we do not know what the "typical" circumstances are in each of the schools, we cannot know if it's fair to compare them. For the purposes of illustrating the value of reflection, let's hypothetically remove some of the variation that is natural in life, but do it equally for both schools. Let's say that both Area High and its neighbor have identical student populations. In both populations, all students have IQs of 100 and come from middle-class families with adequate opportunities for learning inside and outside the home. The children are all physically healthy and well fed. (Sounds like Lake Wobegon, doesn't it?) They have all lived in the community since birth and have all experienced their school's curriculum and instructional practices from year to year.

With all our hypotheticals now in place, what if we were to discover that the students from one high school consistently out-performed the students from the other? With all natural disparities excluded from the equation, the differences in their results would mean that there must be something very different going on in the two schools. The two schools are providing fundamentally different experiences for their students, and those differences have been designed into the two systems in such a way that they are producing *fundamentally* different results.

What might those fundamental differences be? We know that young people who receive systematic instruction and regular practice in reading, writing, and numeracy strategies for learning do better on standardized tests. We also know that children who have the opportunity to learn the content they will be tested on score higher than children who don't learn the material beforehand. Children who apply what they are learning, who are taught how to reason, who read often, who have good vocabularies, and who know how to approach test-taking also do better on standardized measures of achievement (White, 1999).

For these reasons, if our measure of comparison is the ACT or any other standardized test, we should look at the system's design to see whether it consistently provides the instructional emphases described above. It is very likely that in the higher-performing school, these instructional opportunities are built into the whole system in a consistent, cumulative way. In the other school, such opportunities probably are sporadic, perhaps even unintentional, and depend on the teaching staff involved. This fragmentation of instruction, curriculum, and assessment creates massive wholesale variation in a system. When we introduce variation due to differences in the opportunity to learn, we automatically put all our students at a disadvantage.

The differences we removed from this hypothetical case are uncontrollable—educators don't control which families move into our attendance areas, the natural intellectual tendencies of our students, and so forth. But we *can* control the type of educational experiences we provide, and thus minimize the controllable variation in the system.

In fact, it is the job of school boards and central office leaders to minimize controllable variation at the system level so that all students in the district are provided with appropriate learning opportunities and conditions. The only way these leaders can know how much the controllable factors vary is to look at, reflect upon, and learn from data over time. They need a consistent, systematic strategy for reflection to be a key aspect of the system's design.

Monitoring Data Indicators.

We encourage system leaders to use a "dashboard" approach, illustrated in Figure 3.12. This idea involves identifying the primary indicators of system performance and keeping an eye on those indicators from year to year.

Because these leaders know that factors such as learning and achievement status and satisfaction levels will vary somewhat from one year or semester to the next, their monitoring function becomes one of watching these general performance indicators to make sure they remain at acceptable levels. If the system is producing results that consistently fall short of desired levels, it is probably due to the system's design— that is, to common cause variation. To be successful, any improvement strategy launched would have to involve a fundamental system change, such as a change in the design and delivery of staff development activities. If any system indicator

| 3.12 | **Dashboard of Important System Measures** |

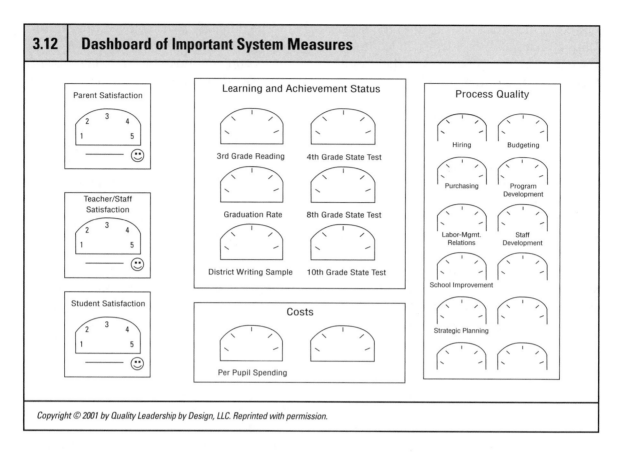

takes an unpredictable, unusual, or dramatic dip or rise, it is likely due to a special cause. The appropriate improvement strategy might be to investigate and resolve the specific problem (such as senior skip day) or, if the specific cause is obviously a one-time "blip" on the radar screen, simply ignore it.

Monitoring Policies and Procedures. Another aspect of reflection on system performance has to do with the policies and procedures that either support or diminish the system's capacity for shared responsibility and continuous improvement. In addition to monitoring data indicators, we encourage board members and others who assist in policymaking to monitor the district's policies and procedures to ensure they are in line with its vision and philosophy. As strategic plans are developed, revitalized, or revised, districts have tremendous opportunity to shift toward a capacity-building model of continuous improvement. Here are some of the questions we believe school boards should address on an ongoing basis:

• What do current policies say about how teachers use their time and the amount of time available for teachers to embrace leadership for learning?

• What kinds of barriers have become embedded within contract language that strip teachers and support staff of their responsibilities and rights to exercise authentic control over their teaching and working environments? (Dolan, 1994)

• What elements of the district's existing policies and procedures support staff, student, and parent engagement in leadership?

• Are procedures for piloting innovations so bureaucratic that they form barriers to change?

• Is the system of standards, curriculum, instruction, and assessment focused, aligned, and capable of self-study? Or are people left to guess about what is expected of them, what the priorities are, and how data might be used if "the real truth" were told?

Creating a Culture for Reflective Practice

The success stories we outline in this chapter are the result of school leaders' intentional efforts to shape a culture in which data are used openly and without fear. Herman and Stringfield (1997) studied educational reform efforts in 25 states and concluded, "The context in which the program was implemented had a great deal of power to facilitate or impede its implementation" (pp. 127–128). Although reflection is not a "program" per se, its introduction is typically accompanied by the same kinds of concerns that arise with any new program or reform initiative.

It is far too easy to jump to conclusions when first viewing data associated with student learning outcomes. Teachers know this well, especially those teachers who have experienced some of the public backlash that arose out of early accountability mandates. Districts must be prepared to deal with the predictable resistance they will face when introducing data and reflection as learning tools. Educator Robert Zemsky (2000) notes that publicizing student learning outcome data often accelerates and even exaggerates political conflict, the likely reason being that "most institutions lack a genuine culture of data" (p. 5).

Let's be blunt: As educators, we've never been particularly good at demonstrating to ourselves or to others that we are achieving the results we desire. In today's highly charged environment of high-stakes testing and accountability, it's not likely we'll embrace the opportunity to use student learning outcomes to publicize our successes unless administrators and board members commit to shaping a culture where data and reflection are valued and where teachers are comfortable and confident using data as means to improve student results. This takes time, patience, and the explicit development of processes that support a learning culture. Herman and Stringfield (1997) concluded from their research that while it is important to consider accountability, the focus on outcomes must be balanced with patience for process.

The process for introducing data and reflection into a system is one important aspect in shaping a culture for continuous learning and improvement. In the successful schools we've studied, teachers' early trepidation about working with data and their concerns about how the data would be used have all but disappeared. Teachers now talk about the *benefits* of this approach. To quote a 7th grade teacher we met, "This process keeps me fresh. It stresses being a professional and the importance of being 'tops.' I have higher standards for and expectations of myself."

These schools are realizing measurable gains in student achievement as teachers and principals incorporate continuous, data-driven improvement into the classroom. When data are used to measure progress against goals at the classroom level, students have a natural model for incorporating continuous improvement into their learning. As one teacher told us, "What we're doing ourselves is what we're trying to do with kids—constant resetting and monitoring of goals and progress. There's a direct translation."

Finally, when teachers can see the results of their actions, they become revitalized. "I find teaching motivating again," one classroom veteran told us. "Using data gets me thinking about new ways to approach things. It's like being a new teacher all over." Ironically, the aspect of the accountability movement that many teachers resist—the measurement of their practice—is what ultimately reconnects them with their reason for entering the profession in the first place.

Common Mistakes to Avoid

Experience has shown us that in their fervor to begin using data for improvement, schools and school districts often make predictable mistakes early in the reflective process. Here are some of the more common examples.

Failure to present data gathering and analysis within the context of the district's overall strategic direction.
In such cases, it appears to teachers that this is just another fad imposed from the outside with little or no purpose other than finding someone to blame.

Failure to explain and show how data will be used.
Why collect data in the first place? Who will see this information? What will they do as a result? Without a "big picture" view of the purpose, process, and application of data gathering and analysis, staff can become increasingly uneasy and unwilling. Districts frequently compound this problem by creating a position that puts an individual in charge of the data. This

"accountability officer" is usually a statistician or technology expert—which further fuels the notion that data are being gathered for the purpose of investigation and inspection rather than learning and reflection. If we leave data in the hands of a chosen few, collaborative learning and improvement cannot occur. Fear, resistance, and suspicion prevail.

Failure to prioritize data gathering and analysis.
Many districts engage in what we refer to as "data dumping"—creating massive piles of numbers, charts, and graphs and believing that all data must be analyzed, understood, and acted upon. Furthermore, these ardent enthusiasts prod beleaguered teachers and administrators to collect even more data, "just in case." This leads to a sense of futility, frustration, and sheer exhaustion as people get buried in data that no one is using.

Easing into Data-Driven Improvement

In one of our recent workshops, we asked teachers to characterize how they currently use data in their practice. One of the veteran teachers proclaimed, "I'm using data to count my days to retirement." This little bit of comic relief was just what was needed to help the group share their issues openly and start thinking about how they could use data within their system.

We have also found that districts tend to be all over the board in terms of their concerns about and readiness for using data for improvement. Many are at the very beginning stages—they have collected data, but they don't know what to do with it. Then there are those districts that have data and can analyze it in rudimentary ways, but are not sure how to translate those numbers action. We also see districts that have used data to identify where improvements are needed, but don't know how to engage staff in the process of collaborative reflection and data-based decision making. These are all perfectly understandable challenges and are easily managed with a little patience, some good processes, and skill development. Here are two useful processes for introducing data and reflection as a positive learning tool.

Process #1: Generate shared guidelines for using data.

In this model, staff develop the guidelines by which everyone agrees to live. Begin by asking the group to think about their concerns related to using data and what it would take to assure them that those concerns would be addressed. Distribute sticky notes and ask all members of the group to write one positive statement that would help assuage their concerns about how data will be used. Collect the statements, grouping similar ideas together as you go. Once all the ideas are heard, the group can add, clarify, or modify the guidelines. Guidelines generated by the schools we've worked with include the following:

- We will handle data with care . . . this is not for "gotcha."
- We will remain open to looking at all the possibilities.
- The purpose of reflecting on data is to create dialogue, which leads to better understanding . . . then to improvement.
- This is an ongoing, continuous, and collaborative learning process.
- We will look at many forms of data before drawing conclusions.
- We will look at data over time whenever possible.
- We'll only collect data based on our need to know.

- We are where we are. We have what we have. Let's make the best of it!

Guidelines like these, when generated collaboratively, help create a common understanding of why and how data will be used. When staff shape the parameters of data gathering and application, they tend to be more comfortable taking on the perceived risks associated with the use of data.

Process #2: Create important conversations that ultimately point out the need for data.

At a regular faculty meeting, devote 15 minutes to small-group discussion focused on a specific question related to student achievement and learning. Point out that the intent of these discussions is not to find the answer in 15 minutes, but to begin an ongoing conversation that might eventually lead to some answers. Here are three conversation starters:

- "How significant is the gap that exists between what we know our students can do and what we expect our students should do?"
- "What is it like to be a child who comes and goes from school to school? What do we need to do to maximize these students' academic growth while they are with us?"
- "What does the data we already have tell us about the performance of our students in the areas we think matter most?"

These kinds of questions guide purposeful data collection and meaningful reflection. When collaborative dialogue focuses on data about student achievement and learning, it helps maintain energy and enthusiasm for the process. The synergies gained from collaborative reflection are best described by Schmoker (1996), who asserts that these kinds of conversations "not only eliminate fear, but also promote team spirit and the uninhibited, continuous knowledge-sharing that are the chief benefits of collective effort. . . . Most of all, data promote the flow of pertinent information and emerging expertise that is the lifeblood of optimism and improvement" (pp. 35–36).

Matching the Data to the Need

Once educators feel safe within the arena of data, it's important for us to understand that not all data are created equal. Matching measurement tools with their appropriate use is akin to selecting the proper tools for a construction project: Pick the wrong tool and the task will be much more difficult and time-consuming. Far worse, selecting the wrong tool can give an inaccurate measurement of the outcome—and lead us to false inferences about student learning.

Uses and Misuses of Standardized Testing

Never has the adage "When all you have is a hammer, everything looks like a nail," been truer than the way in which standardized, norm-referenced tests are often used these days. First, let's consider the purposes and appropriate uses of this kind of measurement tool.

Standardized, norm-referenced tests are designed to give educators information about how students are achieving in core academic areas compared to other groups of students who took the test at the same time under the same conditions. These tests are relatively good measures of facts that have been acquired and retained, assuming that the students taking the test are well fed, thinking clearly, motivated to give it their best, have been exposed to or taught the information being tested, and have some level of skill in taking timed, standardized tests.

The scores and trends that emerge from standardized testing can also provide useful direction to policymakers to the extent that the tests are used to sample student performance (rather than to conduct a mass inspection of the entire population of test-takers) and remain focused on larger systemic issues. An example of an appropriate application of standardized test data might include the decision to reallocate resources to low-performing schools.

Historically, standardized tests have been used as one of several predictors of college success and as such, they are routinely required for college admissions. Although most institutions of higher education now review multiple sources of information about applicants, test scores are almost always among the data considered and are not likely to be eliminated from the battery of admissions requirements any time soon.

We believe standardized, norm-referenced tests can generate good information when they are used in the ways for which they were intended. However, the current political environment has taken the use of this "hammer" to new levels. The hammer has become a sledgehammer! Policymakers are demanding mass inspection—every student tested every year or even twice a year—as if testing *causes* learning. Deming (1982) admonishes us that "routine 100-percent mass inspection to improve quality is equivalent to planning for defects; [it's an] acknowledgment that the process has not the capability required for the specification" (p. 28). Mass inspection neither improves quality nor guarantees quality. It is a costly, unreliable, inefficient, and even counterproductive way to measure or ensure learning.

Increasing the number of times students are tested will not automatically improve their learning. In fact, if policymakers aren't careful, the number of hours students spend taking mandated tests or preparing to take these tests could exceed the number of hours of instruction they receive. Even if all standardized tests were carefully analyzed and used to guide instruction, we would still be able to draw only limited conclusions about instructional effectiveness from student results. Norm-referenced, standardized tests are not particularly good measures of individual student learning.

Additional Data Sources and Measurement Tools

If we wish to know how our children are learning, thinking, and applying their learning, we must move beyond standardized testing by adding to our measurement toolbox and investigating a variety of data sources. The best way to know whether an individual child has truly acquired and internalized knowledge is by observing and assessing his or her performance on authentic tasks and against clear standards and expectations (Newman & Associates, 1996). The general rule of thumb we suggest is the closer you get to the child, the more specific, authentic, and diagnostic your measures should be. Here are some additional guidelines:

• *To measure a state or district's overall capacity and performance.* Use sampling procedures with standardized, norm-referenced tests given every three years or so (typically administered at the 4th, 8th, and 10th grades). Small, scientifically determined samples of standardized test results, monitored through statistical control tools, will provide states and districts with enough information to make effective policy and program decisions at the state and district levels.

• *To determine the progress groups of students are making in particular subject areas or on particular skill sets.* Use scores on local assessment rubrics and classroom assessments, along with the results from standardized, norm-referenced tests. Together, these two forms of measurement provide individual schools, grade levels, departments, and classroom teachers with good information to gauge student achievement and make appropriate instructional decisions.

• *To determine an individual child's needs and strengths.* Use each of the measurement tools cited above in combination with diagnostic tools, student profiles, and portfolios to attain the most complete picture of a child's educational progress. Tailor instruction accordingly.

In addition to test scores and assessment results, schools can learn about important trends in student behavior by examining data such as attendance and truancy rates and the number of disciplinary referrals and actions. Academic indicators that could help determine how well a district or school is performing might include the following:

• Number of National Merit Scholars.

• Amount of scholarship dollars offered to graduates.

• Number of students electing advanced coursework.

• Percentage of students who complete post-secondary education options.

• Dropout, promotion, and retention rates.

• Numbers of students participating in and receiving recognition for outstanding performances at regional, state, or national events.

• Grade point average.

Qualitative data generated from surveys and questionnaires, student observation, interviews, and focus groups can also provide valuable information about levels of satisfaction with the school experience and

3.13	A Guide to Data Sources

Objective	Appropriate Data Sources
Analyze/assess system health and capacity.	Standardized test data over time; customer satisfaction surveys; student behavioral indicators; graduate follow-ups; rates of participation in advanced placement courses; and AP tests taken and passed.
Communicate how a district or school is doing compared to others (nationally, statewide, regionally).	Standardized test data now and over time.
Make curricular modifications at the system level.	Standardized test data; analysis of objectives and levels of mastery by school and district; standards and benchmarks; customized assessments; and graduate follow-ups.
Make curricular and instructional modifications at the classroom/ grade level.	Customized, teacher-developed assessments; district, school, and grade level rubrics; performance tasks; observations; grades; item analysis of some standardized measures; and unit quizzes and tests.
Make resource allocation decisions (i.e., remedial programs, summer school, technology).	Standardized test data over time or with cohort groups; demographic profiles; graduate follow-ups; customer satisfaction surveys; grades; retention patterns; and program evaluations.
Focus on the needs of a specific targeted group of children.	Disaggregated standardized test data; demographic profiles; graduate follow-ups; customer satisfaction surveys; grades; retention patterns; and program evaluations.
Target staff development.	Strategic plan; school goals; school academic performance indicators; trend analysis; surveys; and school, student, and staff demographics profiles.
Make improvements that impact individual student learning.	Customized, teacher-developed assessments; district, school, and grade level rubrics; performance tasks; observations; grades; item analysis of some standardized measures; unit quizzes and tests; running records; and written and oral retellings.

can shed light on school climate, safety, and other environmental aspects of school life.

In short, there are a wide variety of sources and means for gathering and analyzing data. To make the process manageable, educators should begin with an important question, theory, hunch, or need and then decide the kind of data and the measurement tools that will be most useful. Figure 3.13 provides an overview of the purposeful and appropriate use of various data sources and measurement tools. The list is illustrative, not exhaustive.

Summary: Reflection

In this chapter, we have explored the process of *reflection* and the use of data as tools for learning. Individual teachers, grade-level teams and departments, schools, and entire districts benefit when reflection becomes a part of the culture, or, as Deal and Peterson (1999) would put it, "the way we do business around here" (p. 5).

As one of the three supports of our framework, reflection promotes understanding, efficacy, and professional knowledge. It is a critical, core element in a culture of shared responsibility. Reflection stimulates discovery and fuels innovation; as a learning process, it helps educators "tell the truth" about what is working and what is not working.

Sometimes teachers, principals, students, parents, and district administrators like what the data reveal and sometimes the message is hard to take. In all cases, the important thing is that all parties use data to make appropriate adjustments. Reflection allows us to use feedback productively as a means for modifying our behaviors, based on what we are learning about the effect of our actions. Whether or not reflection alerts us to specific problems, the process keeps a school system vital, dynamic, and capable of continuous improvement.

4 Collaboration

> Never doubt that a small group of thoughtful, committed people can change the world. Indeed, it's the only thing that ever has.
>
> —Margaret Mead

"I don't want to feel isolated," says a special education teacher. "I don't want to feel that the burden's only on me. I want to feel that I can collaborate, that my ideas are valued."

Teachers at Auburn Hills Intermediate School have just returned from "Tribes" training and everyone is highly motivated and enthusiastic, ready to implement this team-based program. They are reflecting about how different the school is today from what it was three years ago.

"I used to feel it was totally my responsibility to help students learn, and I didn't think of the child's responsibility in accepting some of that," says a 7th grade teacher. "I've learned to teach in such a way that the child has to have some responsibility, too."

The library media specialist chimes in, "I never used to see myself as a leader. Now I do. And I see my job is to help others—including kids—find the leader within themselves. I focus on bringing people together, making things happen that are good for students."

An 8th grade teacher seems to sum up the sentiment of the group when he says, "If students in another teacher's class don't perform as well as mine, I feel it's my responsibility, too."

Such a strong sense of teamwork and mutual support—of *shared responsibility*—doesn't happen automatically. It requires time, hard work, lots of skill development, good structures and processes for teaming, and leaders who believe their job is to bring out the best in others. In this chapter, we focus on the structures, processes, and skills involved in effective *collaboration*, the third element of our three-part framework for shared responsibility. Within that framework, *focus* represents knowledge and experience; *reflection* represents skillful use of data tools and methods. Collaboration represents the compassionate and wise heart of school improvement. Without collaboration, our knowledge goes unleveraged, our data unused.

The Look, Feel, and Effect of Collaboration

There are many telltale signs of a collaborative environment. Groupings are open, and borders between groups are easily crossed. Parents, students, teachers, support staff, administration, board members, and community members use a common vocabulary to describe what they are trying to achieve together. There is a sense of shared risk as well as success—a feeling that "we're all in this together."

Within a collaborative environment, colleagues visit each other frequently, connecting, observing, and learning from one another. Meetings are energized and productive—and the real meetings happen *in the meetings*, not in the hallways afterward. Information is shared openly and freely, even and especially the "bad news," because it's understood that hiding or distorting information won't lead to real improvement. There is a great deal of respect for innovation and risk taking, and "failures" are seen as opportunities for deeper learning.

People in collaborative environments feel appreciated, valued, and respected; the system brings out the best in them. There is a shared sense of mission and goals; those who are engaged in the organization are there because they choose to be, because they find the school's mission and goals personally compelling, and because they

see their own values reflected in those of the organization.

Does this sound like nirvana? It isn't. Problems *do* arise within collaborative cultures, but they are addressed very differently than they would be in environments where blame, fear, and isolation prevail. People discuss and resolve problems openly rather than behind closed doors. They don't use issues as ammunition for attacking each other. When things go wrong, the question isn't "Who messed up?" but "What is it about our system or our processes that created this problem or failure?"

Research repeatedly stresses the importance of collaboration within school environments and supports strong links between a sense of cooperative community and positive effects on schooling. Particularly for schools working with urban students from struggling families, the development of strong, resilient, collaborative school cultures may mean the difference between success and failure.

A study of 18 high-poverty schools serving "at-risk" youth conducted by the U.S. Department of Education's Office of Educational Research and Improvement concluded that the most effective of these schools are those that are characterized as "caring, cohesive communities" (Shanley, 1999, p. 38). Collaboration was also a distinguishing characteristic of the high-poverty, high-performing schools studied by Gordon Cawelti, who pointed out that teachers in these schools "value the time they have together in teams to improve their practice" (Richardson, 2000, p. 6).

Newmann and Wehlage (1995) also testify to the value of collaboration. In their study of 1400 schools, they discovered, "The most successful schools . . . found a way to channel staff and student efforts toward a clear, commonly shared purpose for student learning; they created opportunities for teachers to collaborate and help one another achieve the purpose; and teachers in these schools took collective—not just individual—responsibility for student learning" (p. 3).

Based on their research into effective professional development practices and high-capacity schools, King and Newmann (2000) contend that for professional development to impact student achievement, it must address three key dimensions: (1) opportunities for sustained learning, (2) collaboration with peers and colleagues both from within and outside the school, and (3) staff development programs that are focused on clear learner goals. They also observe that

> Student achievement is affected most directly by the quality of instruction, which includes the quality of the curriculum, the pedagogy, and the assessment. Instruction is directly affected by school capacity, which includes the total of teachers' knowledge, skills, and dispositions as well as the strength of the professional community and the coherence of the school program (p. 577).

King and Newmann's definition of "professional community" includes:
   • Clear, shared goals (what we call *focus*).
   • Collaboration and collective responsibility for student learning (what we call *collaboration* and *leadership capacity*).
   • Reflective professional inquiry (what we call *reflection*).
   • Opportunities for staff to influence school activities and policies (what we call *leadership capacity*).

This definition of professional community supports the appreciation of collaboration as a powerful element of school improvement. King and Newmann's research into high capacity also underscores how

important it is for schools to define a clear focus supported by reflective, collaborative practices. They found that "whether a school leans more toward 'traditional' or 'authentic' forms of student achievement, high capacity requires strong individual staff competence directed toward focused and sustained collective purposes and supported through reflective collaboration and empowerment of the full staff" (King & Newmann, 2000, p. 578).

Collaboration Skills

Linda Lambert (1998) talks about capacity as "leadership capacity" and defines this as both "broad-based participation" in the work of leadership and "skillful collaboration." *Broad-based participation* means all stakeholders are involved, and *all stakeholders* means teachers, classified staff, administrators, parents/families, community members, and even students. *Skillful collaboration* requires a number of competencies, many of which lie outside educators' traditional training. Figure 4.1 identifies some of the practical skill sets we believe all teachers must have if they are to be skillful collaborators, capable of establishing and sustaining cooperative partnerships.

One of the first steps for schools interested in building collaborative communities is to work these competencies into professional development efforts. But where in the busy school day will we find time first to develop these skills and then to apply them in school improvement efforts?

Finding (and Making) Time for Collaboration

Time—even more than money—is a school's most precious commodity.

| 4.1 | **Educators' Collaborative Training Requirements** |

☑ **Problem-Solving Skills**
- Defining the problem
- Getting to root causes
- Brainstorming solutions

☑ **Decision-Making Skills**
- Building consensus
- Clarifying decision modes and authority
- Using decision matrices

☑ **Communication Skills**
- Listening, advocacy, and inquiry
- Giving and receiving feedback
- Resolving conflict

☑ **Group Process Skills**
- Team building
- Group process observations
- Conflict management

☑ **Meeting Skills**
- Designing and using agendas
- Sharing meeting roles
- Posting ideas

However, if a school hopes to provide effective staff development and improve student results, it must be willing to devote significant time to this undertaking. Staff development that is delivered in 90-minute increments at the end of a tiring school day and is unconnected to the school's improvement goals is like a sheep dip—all the sheep get the same treatment whether they need it (and would benefit from it) or not. And trying to work on school improvement in half-hour intervals is a little like inviting the airplane pilots to step out of the cockpit mid-flight to discuss ways to design a better aircraft. It's just not a smart idea; at the very *least*, you're setting yourself up for a very turbulent ride!

There is simply no getting around the need to set aside concentrated amounts of time for school staffs to come together— away from the distractions of classrooms and cell phones—to develop shared vision and learn new skills. But educators must also restructure our school days and school year and incorporate improvement time as part of the way we "do school." If improvement is not embedded in the daily work of teaching and learning, if it is relegated only to the occasional staff development day and monthly planning council meetings, then schools will always be frustrated by their inability to make significant progress.

The schools that are making significant progress are both making *and* finding time. In a presentation for the Wisconsin Association for Supervision and Curriculum Development's Spring 2000 institute, Linda Lambert pointed out that an interesting phenomenon occurs as leadership capacity grows: Time begins to be perceived less as an enemy (as in "We only have an hour to do this!") and more as an ally (as in "We have an hour together—let's see how much we can accomplish!"). Our own observation is that as skills, vision, and knowledge grow, staffs use time much more productively. Meetings start and end on time and feature fewer interruptions. Goals and outcomes are achieved and people leave meetings knowing what their next steps are. A strong sense of purpose and momentum begins to build.

There are a variety of ways schools can find and make time for ongoing collaboration. The first step is to examine how your school is currently using time in faculty meetings and department and grade-level meetings. Ask yourselves if your meeting agendas are really focusing on improving student learning. Then redesign those agendas to be less about "administrivia" and more about professional development.

School groups can be very creative about how to find time to collaborate. When given the challenge of finding collaboration time without increasing the budget or taking away from student learning, a group from Monona Grove High School brainstormed the following list in just five minutes:

- Combine individual planning time into collaborative time.
- Rearrange specials schedules so that each grade is at specials all together.
- Have previous grade teachers take back their class every two weeks.
- Move the academic start time back one hour and plan meaningful student activities during that time (supervised by noncredentialed staff).
- Create sectionals where support staff take charge of students and discuss issues such as safety, custodial concerns, and cafeteria and food-related topics.
- Hold monthly career exploration days where community members present to students in a large assembly.
- Create an enrichment team of specials and special education/TAG teachers to work with classrooms of students on a rotating basis.

Improvement Time at the School Level

Schools that treat reflection as "how we do business" tend to build time into the school day to allow teams of teachers to examine their data and make plans for improvement. This kind of built-in improvement time is often more difficult to set up in elementary schools than in the middle and high schools; however, we do know of several elementary schools that have established a standard weekly schedule that includes up to an hour of time for teams of same-grade teachers to meet for collaborative work. At one school, classroom teachers meet while their students are entrusted to a team of "enrichment teachers," who have developed units that use art, music, technology, and physical movement activities to expand on what the students are learning in their regular classrooms. In another school, the school's leadership team (which has authority over 80 percent of the school's total budget) decided to hire two "permanent substitute teachers." These teachers participate in the classroom teachers' annual planning activities and understand how to teach every unit. They are available throughout the school year to act as subs while the regular classroom teachers meet for scheduled, ongoing planning time. Because the permanent substitutes are familiar with both the curriculum and the classroom dynamics, they fit seamlessly into the school's instructional program and facilitate rather than disrupt the regular course of student learning.

Improvement Time at the Central Office Level

If the objective is to improve student learning throughout the entire system, the district's central office must also make "improvement time" a valued part of every workweek. It's no secret that many administrative systems are unnecessarily cumbersome and actually get in the way of the "real work" of educating children. Struggling with red tape can drain the life energy out of the school organization and zap its collective will to pursue improvements and innovations. If you ask any member of a school site community—teachers, principal, custodian, food service workers, or school secretaries—what they find most frustrating about the system they work in, chances are good their response will relate to the time lost to bureaucratic paperwork and central office–mandated procedures. In addition to the time these bureaucratic procedures demand, most are fraught with fairly obvious inefficiencies in the form of duplication, rework, and unnecessary wait time—all of which contribute to wasted dollars. The net effect is often a massive, unintentional work slowdown.

Busy people with important things to do don't like to mess with a messy system. That is why in many systems, people have figured out how to circumvent the mess via what we refer to as "work-arounds." *Working around* the system rather than *within* it can save time and money. Unfortunately, work-arounds also have unhappier consequences, such as inconsistencies, inequities, and the generation of more procedural rules designed to catch the clever souls who have found an easier way. Even when teachers, school site administrators, and support staff want to take responsibility for making improvements within their schools and using time wisely, most systems are not flexible enough to allow them to do so.

A very important role for central office administrators and their support staff is to work together to make improvements that will minimize the need for these kinds of work-arounds and simultaneously preserve valuable time necessary to conduct the real business of schools. Figure 4.2 illustrates one time-efficient process for improvement that we recommend highly. Called the Accelerated Improvement Process (AIP), it was developed by the Office of Quality Improvement at the University of Wisconsin, Madison to help teams (such as central

4.2	**The Accelerated Improvement Process**

Meeting 1. Define project scope and purpose (pre-work).

Between meetings—Gather information or data on problems related to purpose and understand the process through flowcharting.

Meeting 2. Focus on possible solutions and the analysis of those solutions, including any data that must be collected from the process' customers. Prioritize solutions.

Between meetings—Collect and analyze data/information on potential solutions.

Meeting 3. Finalize the solutions, incorporate concerns and suggestions raised by customers in the data-gathering phase, and plan for implementation. (At this meeting, the project sponsor learns about the recommendations and agrees to support the implementation plan.)

Adapted with permission from the University of Wisconsin Office of Quality Improvement.

office staffs) make dramatic process and system improvements within a very short period of time—as little as six weeks.

Teams kick off the AIP by identifying a particular problem or goal and end with a formal improvement implementation plan (the actual implementation is handled separately). The process requires staff to hold three meetings—intensive "improvement marathons"—and to perform the majority of the improvement work between meeting sessions. One large, urban school district we know of used the AIP to address and resolve a variety of system problems and make the following improvements:

• The purchasing process, once cumbersome, costly, and complex, was improved so significantly that the district was able to reassign a full-time staff position (40 hours per week) to value-added work in another part of the department.

• The registration and enrollment process, which had involved many variable subprocesses, was streamlined and standardized to provide families and students new to the district with better and more consistent service.

• The hiring process, once multi-layered and lengthy, was revised, cutting the amount of time required to fill an open position from six months to three months. In addition, the district built in procedures to ensure the continuous recruitment of hard-to-hire individuals such as minority teachers and teachers with certifications in special education.

All these improvements were possible because teams of skilled people with knowledge about these processes took the time to meet, to gather data, and to plan and make improvements. The time investment is paying off in the resolution of real problems and in the new availability of resources the district can devote to value-added work.

Improvement Time with Parents

Because so many parents work during the day, finding time to collaborate with them may require schools to adjust teaching schedules and sometimes even contract hours. Matching the amount of time needed with the purpose of the meeting and with the required participants takes skill and thought. We advise schools to first differentiate between those parent-inclusive meetings that need to be concentrated (such as developing shared vision, learning new team skills) and those that will be ongoing (such as checking progress against goals and making budgetary decisions).

Once the distinctions are made, the parent-teacher teams can decide the best way to sort out time issues.

As an example, over the past 10 years, the Madison Metropolitan School District has invested considerable time and thought in how to involve parents in school improvement planning. Many of the district's schools now include parents on steering teams and rely on parents as active participants in visioning sessions. In some cases, parents even participate in school goal setting. District facilitators lend support to ensure activities involving parents are implemented skillfully and efficiently.

Developing Skills Over Time

In our work with high-performing schools, we have been struck by the care the schools' principals have taken to ensure the ongoing development of faculty skills. These principals are finding the balance between assuring teachers that their current knowledge, skills, and expertise are valued and pushing them to expand their boundaries. Marilyn Sudsberry, principal for six years at Forest Dale Elementary in the Carmel Clay District in Carmel, Indiana, recounts how she successfully used collaborative activities to increase staff competence over time.

> Several years before I became principal, the school had a PBA [Performance-based Assessment] on-site visit from the state department of education, and student achievement was found to be low. Not surprisingly, morale was low, too.
>
> When I came on board, people were saying, "Here's another PBA year. What's going to happen this time?" The staff hadn't been looking at test scores at all. Rather than taking them right to the scores, though, I decided to work on the school's culture first. Intuitively, I just

knew they weren't ready for data yet. My vision was to help them create a learner-centered environment.

The first step, in my mind, was to get people collaborating—talking and learning together, creating common vocabulary and knowledge. So we started reading in study groups—we read research reviews of best practices, books about developing learner-centered schools, articles—anything we could get our hands on. As a result, about midway through the year we all had an epiphany: The cafeteria schedule was driving the school! This was just the first "Aha!"

Team skills are essential to effective collaboration—and these skills needed to be developed as a school-community, not just in isolation. So later in the year, we took staff and parents to an intensive team-building workshop. *Then* we began looking at test scores. From there, we developed building-wide learner goals, supported by professional development plans, study groups, action research projects, and journaling/reflective writing. Study teams became a part of the school culture. Staff and faculty meetings moved from focusing on "dit dit administrivia" to staff development and learning.

Now the school holds annual retreats, funded by a combination of PTO funds and grants. We focus on renewing the vision, skill-building around schoolwide goals, and celebrating accomplishments. Over the six years, more and more teacher-leaders have emerged; if you visit the school today, you'll see evidence of collaborative work everywhere.

Marilyn's method for building teacher competence at Forest Dale Elementary demonstrates all three of the factors King and Newman (2000) identify as the most likely to promote teacher learning. Staff development efforts were sustained, involved collaboration with peers and colleagues both from within and outside the school, and focused on clear learner goals.

Additionally, Forest Dale's example shows that when teachers increase their competence through collaboration, student learning tends to increase as well.

Lowell Elementary School Principal Sue Abplanalp also understands the connections between staff development, collaboration, and improved student learning. Over the past three years, Sue has studied the effect of her school's staff development on student results and on teachers' capacity to integrate best practices. She began by asking teachers to identify skill and knowledge areas they would like to learn more about and ways they would like to learn; then, she focused staff development on what the teachers were ready to do. Next, Sue developed a "rubric of change" based on Michael Fullan's (1991) change process steps of *inquiry, initiation, implementation,* and *institutionalization.* Then she tracked teachers' abilities to implement best practices in math, reading, and writing literacy.

The results? When Sue launched this process, just 12 of Lowell's 33 teachers had institutionalized best practices in their classrooms. Today, after 3 years of extensive staff development incorporating collaborative learning time, 31 of 33 teachers are either implementing or have already institutionalized the changes.

Lowell's gains in student achievement are equally impressive. Three years ago, only 25 percent of 4th grade students achieve scores of proficient or above on the state math test; less than 20 percent scored proficient or above on the state writing test. Today over 70 percent of Lowell's 4th graders test as proficient or above in math and 60 percent test as proficient or above in writing.

Both Marilyn Sudsberry and Sue Abplanalp see staff development as key to building collaborative, results-oriented staff

4.3	Staff Development Options

Which of these could be effective methods of staff development?

❑ Afterschool workshops
❑ Peer coaching/mentoring
❑ Informal peer observation
❑ Conference attendance
❑ Action research
❑ Presentation by visiting consultant
❑ Teacher collaboration for lesson planning
❑ Faculty meeting with instructional strategy sharing
❑ Ongoing study groups/learning teams
❑ Faculty meetings

attitudes. Which of the options listed in Figure 4.3 do you think they would identify as constituting "effective staff development?" Take a moment and check all that apply.

For both principals, the answer would be "all of the above." High-performing schools characteristically incorporate staff development methods into the work of the school; the methods they choose honor and build staff expertise and focus on the goal of improving student learning and achievement.

Structural Changes that Support Collaboration

Schools wanting to institute effective collaboration should also examine their established structures for working together. Those that have developed collaborative cultures use both ad hoc and ongoing teams to get work done. *Ad hoc teams* are those that spring up to focus on specific problems or challenges and then disband when the problem is resolved or the challenge is met. *Ongoing teams* are established and remain in place to address recurring functions or needs. Figure 4.4 contrasts the features of these different work group types and lists typical examples of each.

When creating a team environment, it's important to pay attention to the different types of support ad hoc and ongoing teams will require. For example, ad hoc teams need to spend relatively more time defining their mutual interests in a shared mission or purpose. They tend to struggle more with issues of time, workload, and the distribution of responsibilities. They also need clear criteria for determining when their work is complete. Some of the school districts we've visited have had more than 80 teams going at once, fully two-thirds of which had "finished" their tasks but hadn't yet disbanded!

Ongoing teams need a different type of support. The team's mission is usually clear to all members; however, because ongoing teams meet so frequently, members have a tendency to get distracted by nonvital tasks. It is particularly helpful for these groups to make sure each meeting agenda reflects a clear purpose and is designed to produce outcomes that are important work, not just administrivia. Ongoing teams also tend to develop strong inner-group cultures that can act as barriers to newcomers. It is important that these teams use strategies for remaining open to outside information, otherwise they risk developing an insular kind of group arrogance ("We know what we know and have always known").

Many elementary schools are having great success with a "cadre system," a collaborative arrangement in which cross-sectional teams (teams formed across grade levels) gather weekly to compare

4.4	**Ad Hoc and Ongoing Teams**	
Type of Team	**Characteristics**	**Examples**
Ad Hoc	• Have a beginning and an end • Members may come and go • Have a specific, usually stated, purpose or goals • Often include members of various disciplines, functions, or perspectives • Members often feel a "first allegiance" to other parts of the organization	• Curriculum program improvement teams • Problem solving teams • Action research teams • Process improvement teams • Study circles
Ongoing	• Exist "for the duration" • Membership is relatively stable • May or may not have a stated mission, but do have a purpose • Often include members sharing similar perspectives or functions • Members usually feel "first allegiance" to this team	• Grade, subject, departmental teaching teams • School leadership teams • Curriculum direction and alignment teams

curriculum to standards, reflect on student assessment data, and plan improvements.

One such example can be found at Mendota Elementary School, where a "teachers-helping-teachers" philosophy is in place. At Mendota, the principal, Title I coordinator, social worker, school psychologist, and technology coordinator attend each cadre meeting. Principal Sandy Gunderson explains:

> At first, our school was more principal-modeled because it felt "high risk" to teachers to share with each other what was working and not working in their classrooms. As competency increased with coaching and inservice training, the quality of questions improved. Now there's more focus on student learning in these meetings and less focus on concrete nuts-and-bolts like field trips.

Mendota's teachers-helping-teachers model is working, and the school's high degree of technology integration is one form of evidence. The technology coordinator, a regular participant in cadre planning work, regularly demonstrates standards-based, integrated curricular units for the teachers and students, and then provides guidance and support for teachers as they lead the units in their own classrooms. At this school, technology and information literacy standards are fully integrated with the curriculum standards, and each student has an electronic portfolio, which shows year-to-year gains in both content and technology competencies.

Another example of effective team structures can be found at Sennett Middle School. For more than 20 years, the school has been organized as a "house" system, with students assigned to a house for three years. Classrooms are multi-age, with 6th, 7th, and 8th graders learning together. Each teacher serves on a curriculum cadre specializing in math, science, social studies, or communications. Some of the teachers—experts in reading, writing, and technological literacy—spend one half of the school day teaching solo and the other half teamed with colleagues to model specific lessons, lead a targeted group through a particular unit, or help plan new units. In recent years, the school has added two special education teachers to each of its house teams; the special education teachers help differentiate instruction for *all* students.

Sennett Middle School's house teaching teams meet several times a week during common planning time to discuss upcoming curriculum, consult about individual student learning and behavioral issues, review assessment data, and plan new units. The house team teachers are responsible for students' instructional placements and groupings throughout the year (they generally favor a flexible grouping approach). House teachers also plan frequent instructional activities that involve the entire house, thereby reinforcing a sense of community across the whole group.

Sennett uses a standards-based thematic curriculum that rotates on a three-year basis. Each summer, teams of teachers meet to develop, update, and continually improve the curriculum (and they receive extra compensation for this work). The school's unified arts teachers—art, music, physical education, and technology—further enhance the curriculum by working collaboratively with the classroom teachers to tie instruction to the thematic units.

How has all this collaborative effort affected Sennett's students? Although the school has long been known for its collaborative team culture, the addition of a focus on results coupled with data-driven reflection has helped students achieve at higher levels. The numbers speak clearly. Within three years, Sennett's lower-SES 8th graders increased their percentage of proficient/advanced scores on the state's reading test from 24 percent to close to 60 percent. The number of students scoring at the minimal level in reading decreased from 19 percent to 10 percent. As Principal Jan Dowden explains, "People now see the clear, direct results of all their efforts. They see the true value of collaboration: its impact on instructional improvement and student achievement."

Changing Habits of Mind

Putting collaborative teaming structures in place does not in itself change longtime habits of mind. In many cases, before schools can build shared responsibility for student learning, they must reexamine their beliefs and assumptions about the value of collaborative school cultures. Despite public education's origins in the ideals of democracy and equity, historically, school systems have not been organized along collaborative lines. For well over a century, the norm—the rule, even—has been the hierarchical structure of the school board that oversees the administration that oversees teachers. Many school cultures still reflect the traditional organization, which includes the following characteristics:

• A principal who is "in charge" of the school and of working with parents and the community.

• Teachers who are "in charge" of their individual classrooms. Each teacher decides what students should learn, how they should learn it, and how they will be assessed and evaluated.

For principals and teachers long accustomed to being in charge, a move toward a collaborative culture can present some difficulty. Collaboration requires us to surrender some of our control. It also requires us to be open to others' perspectives and to be willing to find out that perhaps we don't always know "the right answer" or "the best answer." This can be particularly threatening when parents are invited into the process as equal partners—in the past, as educators we've been accustomed to positioning ourselves (and being positioned) as "the experts" when it comes to making decisions for children's learning. In a collaborative culture, we need to turn to knowledge and skills rather than licenses and degrees—and be able to admit that sometimes we just don't know.

Perhaps the most difficult part about changing our attitudes about collaboration lies in our fear of demonstrating our own ignorance, which we interpret as incompetence. Surely, as professionals, *incompetent* is the worst label we can place on our colleagues or ourselves. Here's how one principal we talked with summed up the risk associated with the "openness" of collaboration:

> It's hard for teachers to move out of that classroom—to open that door. Now they're accountable to each other and there are equity issues, and they have to share. You are exposing competency—we have "competency hot buttons" all over us. If we don't respect that, we see all the anxiety just flying.

One of the most important ways to overcome fear and bolster collaboration is through conversations about *focus*—the school's core values, purpose, and vision. These topics help individuals talk about what everyone has in common (a concern for student learning), rather than dwelling on what makes them different, and thus "not to be trusted." Such conversations often lead to a clearer understanding of the things that set groups apart, which helps to break down intergroup barriers.

Overcoming "Tribal" Behaviors

In her book *Tribal Warfare in Organizations* (1988), organization consultant and anthropologist Peg Neuhauser documents the dynamics of intergroup conflict. She observes that groups within organizations tend to affiliate by jobs or shared duties. These "tribes" develop their own special terminology, traditions, symbols, and rituals, all of which essentially constitute separate cultures. Unless there are intervening processes to pull these disparate groups together, each will act only on its own behalf.

Within a school setting, it would not be unusual for tribes of teachers, support staff, administrators, parents, and students to be acting out agendas that are very different from one another. Each tribe seeks to maximize its own resources and meet its own needs, without considering the part it plays in the greater whole. This kind of tribal behavior can even be seen in the "cultures" of the various academic disciplines. For example, have you ever listened to members of the science department talk about the value of the English department or vice versa?

A few years ago, we attended a National Institute for Science Education Interdisciplinary Teamwork Symposium featuring researcher Leona Schauble. Speaking about her experience developing child-focused television segments in collaboration with producers from The Children's Television Workshop and curators from The Children's

Museum of Indianapolis, Schauble observed that the most successful interdisciplinary collaborators tend to be those who are willing to take on (at least provisionally) the perspectives, values, and goals of their colleagues. She found that the most effective producers were those who began to be able to think like researchers, and the most successful researchers were those who began to think like producers. The name Schauble used to describe these successful collaborators has stuck with us; she called them "bridge people."

The ability to see the world from another's perspective and act as bridge people requires us to suspend our own judgments, stereotypes, and even values. Growing up in a culture that values debate and discussion, winners, and independent entrepreneurs, many of us possess an unfortunate handicap when it comes to developing this ability. But as we move toward creating *shared* purpose—one that incorporates multiple diverse points of view—this ability becomes priceless.

Physicist David Bohm studied group conversation to identify the various ways that groups create meaning. The originator of the process of "dialogue," Bohm observed that in most conversations, people tend to take up individual positions, which they will defend unswervingly. The skills of *debate* (to "break down" or "take apart") and *discussion* (from the root *discus* meaning "to hurl or throw") do little to create common purpose; rather, they tend to entrench us more firmly in our original positions.

On the other hand, the art of dialogue (from *dia* meaning "through" and *logos* meaning "the word") involves creating shared meaning through words. Bohm writes, "In a dialogue there is no attempt to gain points, or to make your particular view prevail. It is more a common participation, in which people are not playing a game against each other but with each other. In a dialogue everybody wins" (1992, pp. 16–18). In dialogue, the ideas provide the nourishment for the interaction. It is a creative, generative process, out of which we hope to gain a new and shared understanding.

Dialogue requires two complimentary skills: advocacy and inquiry.

• *Advocacy* is our ability to make our thinking and reasoning visible to others as we test our assumptions and conclusions. For example, in talking with other teachers about what to emphasize in skill development, a teacher might say, "I think our students are not learning enough about how to formulate problems. I say this because I see the evidence in their writing and their reasoning and problem solving math scores. What do the rest of you think about this?"

• *Inquiry* is our ability to ask questions that will help others make their thinking visible, so that we may compare our assumptions to theirs. In the example above, a member of the group might respond, "What leads you to that conclusion? I'm asking because I'm wondering about the connection you see between problem formulation, writing, and math. . . ."

It's important to note that in the process of dialogue, advocacy is not about proving a point or trying to convince others to adopt your perspective; rather, it involves suspending certainty that you are right and taking interest in creating new and better meaning. Similarly, inquiry is not about "gotcha"—about proving errors in others' thinking; its purpose is to deepen understanding of an issue, problem, or challenge. Figure 4.5, adapted by Robert Garmston and Bruce Wellman (1999) from Senge's *The Fifth Discipline Fieldbook*, provides a useful

4.5	**Advocacy and Inquiry in Dialogue**

Use Advocacy . . .	**Use Inquiry . . .**
✓ **To make your thinking and reasoning visible.**	✓ **To ask others to make their thinking visible to you.**

Use Advocacy . . .

✓ **To make your thinking and reasoning visible.**

State your assumptions: "Here's what I think, and here's how I got there."

Describe your reasoning: "I came to this conclusion because. . . ."

Distinguish data from interpretation: "This is the data I have as objectively as I can state it. Now here is what I think the data mean. . . . "

Explain the context: "Several groups would be affected by what I propose and here is how. . . ."

Give examples: "To get a clear picture, imagine that you are in school X. . . ."

✓ **To test your assumptions and conclusions.**

Encourage others to explore your model, assumptions, and data: "What do you think about what I just said? Do you see any flaws in my reasoning? What can you add?"

Reveal where you are least clear: "Here's one area you might help me think through. . . ."

Stay open: Encourage others to provide different views: "Do you see it differently?"

Search for distortions, deletions, and generalizations: "In what I've presented, do you believe I might have over generalized or left out data or reported data incorrectly?"

Use Inquiry . . .

✓ **To ask others to make their thinking visible to you.**

Gently walk others down the ladder of inference: "What leads you to that conclusion? What data do you have for that?"

Use unassertive language and an approachable voice: "Can you help me understand your thinking here?"

Draw out their reasoning: "What is the significance of that? How does this relate to your other concerns? Where does your reasoning go next?"

Explain your reasons for inquiring: "I'm asking about your assumptions here because. . . ."

Invite introspection: "What questions do you have about your thinking?"

✓ **To compare your assumptions to the assumptions of others.**

Investigate other assumptions: "Would you be willing to each list our assumptions, compare them, and explore if there might be other assumptions surrounding this issue?"

Confirm your understanding by paraphrasing and probing: "Am I correct that you are saying. . . ."

Test what they say by asking for broader contexts or examples: "How would your proposal affect. . . ? Is this similar to. . . ? Can you describe a typical example?"

Reveal your listening processes: "I have been listening for themes. So far I've heard two. Are there others?"

Adapted by permission of the publisher from The Adaptive School: Developing and Facilitating Collaborative Groups *by Robert Garmston and Bruce Wellman. Copyright © 1999 Christopher-Gordon Publishing.*

tool for using advocacy and inquiry in dialogue-based conversations.

The process of dialogue is helpful any time people gather to solve a problem or produce something new. It proves useful when discussing the quality of student work, developing results-oriented goals, creating values-based vision, resolving conflicts, and developing innovative programs. Dialogue skills are essential to schools, districts, and communities that are committed to building shared responsibility for student learning. Through dialogue, we can communicate our respect for data and relationships, bridge tribal divides, and create new meaning around our shared purpose.

Understanding and Promoting Community Development

Every group—even one with impeccable dialogue skills—will travel through predictable stages of development as it evolves from a collection of individuals to a highly collaborative, high-performing community (Jewell & Reitz, 1981; Peck, 1987). These stages, illustrated in Figure 4.6, apply to *any* group at *any* level—whether it is a cadre of teachers, a department, a steering team, or an entire school.

An awareness of these stages can help group members feel less anxious about group relations ("What we're going through

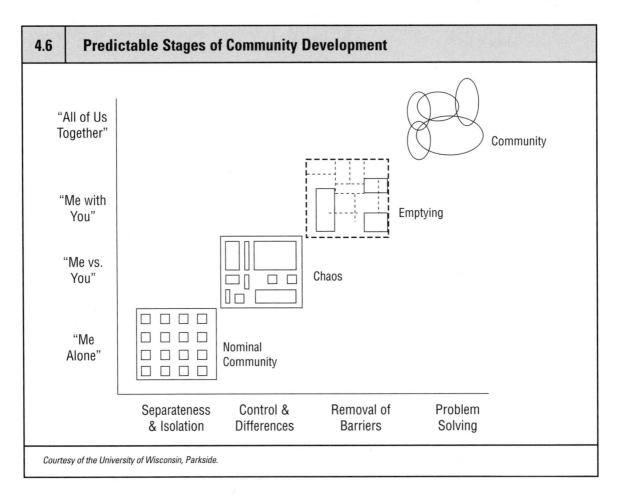

4.6	Predictable Stages of Community Development

"All of Us Together"

"Me with You"

"Me vs. You"

"Me Alone"

Community

Emptying

Chaos

Nominal Community

Separateness & Isolation   Control & Differences   Removal of Barriers   Problem Solving

Courtesy of the University of Wisconsin, Parkside.

is normal!") and show them what they need to do to further the group's progress. Let's take a closer look at each stage.

The Nominal Community Stage

When groups first come together, they are a community in name only. This initial stage is something like an orientation period, and because no one knows quite what to expect, there can be confusion and uncertainty and maybe even some anxiety. Some members may be very excited; others may not. Roles are changing, people are learning new skills, and that learning can be frustrating.

Groups in the first stage of development tend to look for easy answers, quick fixes, and external solutions. Members discuss issues in a general way, but they do not share their individual experiences or explain how events affect them personally. Intergroup relationships are characterized by conflict avoidance. All members are individually preoccupied by the question of how they fit into the group and whether the others will accept them. Seeking community, they tend to emphasize their similarities and either ignore or gloss over their differences and disagreements. The group avoids heated argument and debate, and conflicts usually remain underground, where they can sometimes fester destructively.

The group members who have the easiest time during the nominal community stage are those who have faith in a collaborative philosophy and are personally committed to building effective communities. These are the people who look for the small successes the group can build on, communicate the little victories, and give positive feedback. They don't look for the failures (which are inevitable); they don't find reasons for why ideas will never work. They

reframe problems as challenges and opportunities and help the group to build a sense of collective strength from individual and diverse skills.

The main agenda for groups in the nominal community stage is to address the issues of mission, vision, goals, and expectations, and to clarify the tasks they will undertake. This is also the time to establish a set of *ground rules* for how group members will work together. Figure 4.7 lists topics we recommend groups address in their ground rules. A good set of ground rules (which should be reviewed occasionally and changed if necessary) will promote efficient group operation and collective understanding; they will also serve as an important reference point when the group inevitably moves on to the next stage, *chaos*.

The Chaos Stage

As groups begin to develop common expectations, members go through a period of frustration and disagreement. Significant conflicts typically arise around issues of leadership, power, control, and influence. Members wrestle with the questions of how much relative influence they will exert on the team and who they will allow to influence them. There may be a "power struggle" between dominant members.

During the chaos stage, intergroup relationships are characterized by mistrust and turmoil. Disagreements tend to open, and the airing of long-standing differences can lead to fragmentation, even polarization. Members take sides or join "camps" and become intent on defending their own positions or turf. They listen to opposing views only long enough to derive ammunition for the next round of debate. Gossip, backbiting, and scapegoating can become the norm. Name-calling and personal

4.7	**Suggested Topics for Ground Rules**

Attendance
If someone is unable to attend a meeting, should he or she send an alternate? Will meetings be held if more than ___ (#) are unable to attend? Is to OK to miss more than ___(#) meetings?

Promptness
Will the meeting begin even if not everyone is present yet? How will a late participant be brought up to speed?

Equal opportunity to participate
How will members ensure that everyone has a chance to "share the air" in discussions?

Interruptions
Can the meetings be interrupted by phone calls?

Conversational courtesies
Are side conversations OK? Is interrupting a speaker OK?

Assignments
Will everyone expect to take on some responsibilities between meetings? Will subteams be assigned?

Decision making
How will key decisions be made? By consensus? What if the group cannot reach consensus?

Confidentiality
Is it all right to tell other people outside this meeting what we talked about? Will sensitive issues be of concern?

Meeting evaluation
Will we periodically review our meetings to see if they are efficient and effective?

---

attacks can even arise, deepening members' feelings of mistrust and risk.

Attempts to get out of the chaos and turmoil can include cutting off debate or discussion, either by decree or through intellectualizations, generalizations, and abstractions. Some members try to flee back into the pseudo-safety of the nominal community stage; others leave the conflict and retreat into isolation.

Despite the ugliness of this stage, chaos in some form or other is an essential phase in building community and teamwork. The problem is not the presence of chaos, but rather, the risk of getting stuck there. As Robert Frost put it, "The only way out is through." A group's critical task at this stage is to resolve the issue of how it will define "leadership" and how it will distribute work.

It's also essential to clarify member roles, responsibilities, and spheres of influence. A group's strongest tools for navigating through the chaos and advancing to the next stage of development are its mission and vision and its original ground rules.

The Emptying Stage

As member roles are clarified, groups move through a period when they resolve a variety of conflicts and issues and establish behavioral norms. Members "empty" themselves of grievances, abandon old allegiances and attitudes, and begin to participate as active players on the new team. Functional relationships emerge as individuals begin to negotiate disagreements, understand their own strengths and weaknesses within in the group, and gain a better idea of when they should lead and when they should follow.

The use of dialogue is key to moving through the emptying stage. (Some groups have found the Historygram exercise discussed in Chapter 2 an effective way to let go of the past.) As the group continues to move forward, members remove barriers to authentic and mutual communication. People abandon abstractions, begin to speak more personally, and share their own experiences. They let go of their defensive stances—their need to be right, to prevail, or to hold their position—and instead focus on finding the best solutions.

The Fully Functioning Community Stage

As groups mature, they enter the stage where they can focus on performance and results, and act as a fully functioning, cohesive community. Members are realistic in their expectations. In this stage, the group becomes very efficient. With major conflicts resolved and behavioral norms clarified, they are free to direct attention toward achievement. Productivity and continued community building are now the primary issues. Cooperation replaces competitiveness. Members work together in constructive ways to achieve common goals.

When a group discovers a sense of community, it often experiences a burst of creative energy. Members replace self-defeating behaviors with unexpected and even brilliant solutions. Barriers that had seemed insurmountable become manageable. Diversity is respected and honored. Leadership is spontaneous and comes from anyone in the group, regardless of "official" role or position. Conflicts are expected, so when they arise, they are not allowed to fester, but are dealt with immediately, openly,

authentically, and respectfully. The group generates great self-confidence through its successes. In the fully functioning community stage, members can develop a bond that makes their group feel invincible.

Navigating the Stages

Although all groups generally go through all four stages of development, the rate at which they do so may vary, depending on the group's size, the mission's complexity, the members' personalities, and a host of situational specifics. Groups can develop faster if they are given the appropriate training, time to deal with issues, and leadership support along the way.

It's important to note that progression through the stages is not always a straight line. All sorts of external factors can influence community development, and groups may find themselves repeating stages, even "moving backward." Teams might lose or add significant numbers of members, for instance; they might find that their primary mission has been redefined; there might even be a total break-up of the community. Any of these changes will have a major impact on the group and will force members to readdress their fundamental expectations, goals, norms, and ground rules. Group members may initially be discouraged at this perceived "backsliding," but once the phenomenon is accepted, they can begin working together to regain the fully functioning community stage.

We also want to stress that "community" is not an end stage; it is a dynamic, working discipline that requires constant practice. The four stages of development are neither stagnant nor permanent. Moments of chaos will inevitably arise in all groups. But real communities are reflective. They will recognize the movements they experience, discuss them, and find ways to regain their functionality. The price of staying stuck in *nominal community* or *chaos* can be a loss of physical and mental health; the reward for *emptying* and moving toward being a *functional community* is the great satisfaction that comes from working together at high levels of performance and learning.

We recommend that beginning groups in particular spend time getting to know these stages and develop plans for what they will do when they reach each stage. In Chapter 2's discussion of focus, we explored the importance of developing core values that will guide the work of the school community. Many groups have taken this farther by defining specific guidelines for how they wish to treat one another in a collaborative community. We provide a sample set of group guidelines in Figure 4.8. These 10 rules represent one group's commitment to make the work they do together as enjoyable and productive as possible. These guidelines can be easily modified and can help any group navigate through the predictable stages of becoming a collaborative community.

Summary: Collaboration

The teachers we heard from at the beginning of this chapter were reflecting on the changes they went through during Auburn Hills Intermediate School's transformation from a culture where isolation and anxiety reigned to one where collaboration and trust are the rule. When you look beyond the specifics they cite—their talk of data, student results, and improved accountability—you can see the essential lesson they've learned: *Relationships count and people matter.* As the special education teacher said toward the end of the meeting, "I need to feel

4.8	Ten Guidelines for Effective Group Work

1. Be critical of ideas, not individuals.
2. Participate and master all relevant information.
3. Be willing to take leadership in areas where the group needs help.
4. Listen and sincerely try to understand everyone's ideas, even if you don't agree.
5. Paraphrase to check on your understanding of what someone has said.
6. Bring out all ideas before trying to put them together or evaluate them.
7. Don't be afraid to change your mind if new information warrants it.
8. Share information openly.
9. Keep your eye on the goal of making the best decision possible—not on looking good or winning.
10. Remember, *we're all in this together.*

we have a relationship, that we really get to know each other so we can have rapport that allows us to feel that we understand each other's needs. I'll do almost anything if it's appreciated enough. That's important to me."

We have now talked about the three supports for our framework for shared responsibility. In the next chapter, we will focus on goal setting as a way to pull these three elements together. We'll show you how your school can combine *focus, reflection,* and *collaboration* to establish a learning process that builds leadership capacity and, as a result, supports shared responsibility for student learning.

5 SMART Goals

*The one accomplishment that would foster longer-range actions would be
a goal worthy of commitment.*

—Peter Senge, *The Fifth Discipline* (1990)

The Verona Area School District is known throughout the state of Wisconsin for its commitment to site-based governance and to providing school choice within its system. Having spent 10 years establishing a culture of collaboration, dialogue, and choice, in 1995 the district made a further commitment to use data-driven decision making to improve student results and began learning the SMART* goal setting process as a vehicle for implementation in schools and classrooms. The paired schools Stoner Prairie Elementary (K–2) and Savanna Oaks Elementary (3–5) were the first to pilot the process at the classroom level.

The 5th grade art teachers at Savanna Oaks opened that school year with the following "Art SMART" goal: "By the end of this semester, increase by 10 percent the number of 5th grade students that meet or exceed expectations for realistic hand drawing." Figure 5.1 shows the rubric these teachers developed to help them assess their students' skills and monitor student progress toward the goal.

When a few of the classroom teachers objected to using a SMART goal in art class (claiming "it destroys the aesthetic process!"), one of the art teachers demurred. "We teach skills, too," she said. "It's important that students and their parents see this growth." The art teachers went on to develop a plan for teaching the skills involved in real life drawing and used the rubric as an ongoing assessment tool to monitor student progress on the SMART goal.

As Figure 5.2 shows, the students and their parents did see growth—more than enough growth to meet the teachers' Art SMART goal. The 5th graders'

---

*"SMART" = Specific and Strategic, Measurable, Attainable, Results-oriented, and Timebound. See O'Neill, 2000a.

5.1	**Rubric for Art Class**	
Place your non-drawing hand on the table in front of you. Draw your hand.	Place your non-drawing hand on the table in front of you. Draw your hand.	Place your non-drawing hand on the table in front of you. Draw your hand.
		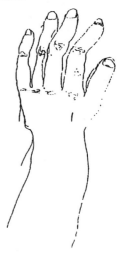
Pre-Instruction Does not meet expectations	Pre-Instruction Meets Expectations	Pre-Instruction Exceeds Expectations

Courtesy of Savanna Oaks Elementary School, Verona, Wisconsin.

post-instruction drawings showed 50-percent fewer students in the "does not meet expectations" category and a 19-percent increase in the "exceeds expectations" category. The art teachers felt a great deal of pride in sharing these results with their colleagues; the improvement in students' drawing skills confirmed the art teachers' instructional efforts had been effective.

Given this experience of success—of setting an important goal and meeting it—chances are good that these 5th grade art teachers will continue to improve their practice and become even more effective instructors. As teacher efficacy researchers Tschannen-Moran and colleagues (1998) write, "Mastery or enactive experiences are the most powerful source of efficacy information. The perception that a performance has been successful raises efficacy beliefs, which contributes to the expectation of proficient performance in the future" (p. 229).

This feeling of *efficacy*, the belief that what one does makes a difference, is at the center of building shared responsibility for student learning; the process of using goals to improve one's practice and one's school is the engine.

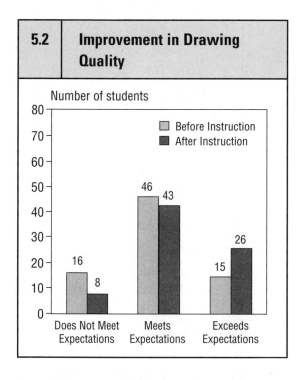

5.2	**Improvement in Drawing Quality**

Number of students

In previous chapters, we have emphasized the need to integrate *focus, reflection,* and *collaboration* to build shared responsibility for student success. Nowhere is that integration more important than in developing and using goals to guide your school, classroom, or district performance. In this chapter, we first examine the difference between "results goals" and "process goals," then describe how to make goals "SMART." We conclude by examining SMART goal processes at the classroom, school, and district levels, and showing how these goals can help build focused, reflective, and collaborative communities where all members know they make a difference.

Choosing the Right Kind of Goals

Rosenholz (1991) tells us that goals are the "center to the mystery of school's success, mediocrity or failure" (p. 13). But goals come in many shapes and sizes, types and functions. When we set out to develop goals for our classrooms, schools, and districts, what kind of goals should we set?

Let's start by thinking about Peter Senge's statement at the opening of this chapter: "The one accomplishment that would foster longer-range actions would be *a goal worthy of commitment.*" What educational goals can we identify as being "worthy of commitment"? Closing the achievement gap? Creating more innovative, engaging schools? Increasing parent involvement? Eliminating school violence?

Each of these goals "sings" to us for different reasons. If you examine your reactions to these goals, you'll probably find that you react based on your beliefs, values, and vision about the purpose (the mission) of public education. Similarly, all district, school, and classroom goals should be rooted in our missions, visions, and values.

When educators have devoted care and attention to creating shared vision, when we have undertaken a thorough assessment of the "gaps" between our current situation and our vision for the future, and when we have identified the "vital few" strategic priorities we will use to close these gaps, then developing goals that are personally and communally meaningful is a natural next step. Yet making sure goals are meaningful and heartfelt isn't enough to ensure continuous improvement of student learning. Goals must also be *specific* and they must be *measurable.* For many of us in education, these last two provisos are foreign concepts.

Understanding Process Goals and Results Goals

Suppose you visited one high school that had goals of "implementing an integrated math/science program for incoming freshmen" and "adopting a zero tolerance policy toward violence." Next, you visited a high school that had goals of "reducing the failure rate of incoming freshmen" and "eliminating violent behaviors." Although at first glance the two sets of goals seem similar, a closer look reveals they are really very different.

The first school has established goals that define the activities it hopes will contribute to positive outcomes. This type of goal, expressed in the form of programs or policies, is called a *process goal*. The second school's goals define not its planned activities, but its desired outcomes—in this example, a lower rate of failure and no incidences of violence. The second school's goals are *results goals* and are identifiable as such because they answer the "so what?" question: "So what if we did X, Y, and Z? What actual improvement would we see?"

Both goal-types have value, but each serves a distinctly different purpose. As Figure 5.3 shows, process goals identify the methods, actions, and activities school staffs can use to build their capacity for improvement. Results goals identify what all that capacity building adds up to.

Educators looking for effective tools to measure performance and progress need goals that are results-oriented rather than process-oriented (see Rosenholz, 1991; Schmoker, 1998). We need goals that identify what we desire in terms of performance *after* or *as a result of* putting new processes in place or improving existing processes. However, our field experience confirms what many researchers have found: Most educational goals are related to processes, not results, and are geared toward establishing and executing activities, programs, and instructional methods.

It's true that process goals aimed at improving education might "foster longer-range actions" (to quote Senge again) and therefore be "worthy of commitment," but

5.3	Process Goals and Results Goals
Process Goals *focus on...*	**Results Goals** *focus on...*
Means	Ends
Inputs	Outputs
Capacity improvements	Productivity
System interventions	Outcomes
Improvement activities	Improvement targets
Function	Purpose

Copyright © 2001 by Quality Leadership by Design, LLC. Reprinted with permission.

how would we know for sure? To illustrate, a process goal like "implementing an integrated math/science curriculum for incoming freshmen" is a strategy and very likely a necessary part of an action plan. But this goal does not tell us what level or performance, what *outcome*, we should expect this integrated math/science curriculum to bring about. It provides no answer to the "so what" question. In addition, without *measurable* results to work toward, "meeting the goal" is simply a matter of checking items off a list. Say that our school implements the integrated math science curriculum; we've met our goal, but what have we really accomplished? How do we know if what we've put in place has truly made a difference in student learning?

Transforming Processes into Results

The problem is not that educators *use* process goals; after all, we need processes to build our capacity for improvement. No, the problem lies in having *only* process goals, with no goals that measure the effectiveness of the processes we put in place. The truth is, we need both processes *and* results.

For every process goal you set, you should be able to answer the "so what?" question with the desired result. So what if we put this process in place? What would be the ultimate purpose or the improvement? Figure 5.4 provides examples of how answering the "so what" question can transform process goals into results goals that are specific and measurable.

Getting SMART

Having focused on how to make goals more results-oriented, let's now explore how we can also make them SMART: specific and strategic, measurable, attainable, results-

oriented, and timebound (O'Neill, 2000a). SMART goals provide educators with the means to develop feedback on which of our efforts are making a difference and by how much. For example, here's a SMART goal from a high school: "Within the next two years, reduce by 50 percent the number of students needing remedial reading assistance after 9th grade (over the past five years, 20 to 30 students have required this assistance)." This goal is

• *Specific and strategic.* It focuses on students in grades 10 to 12 and it deals with reading skills, a strategic priority in the district.

• *Measurable.* The school knows how many students have required assistance in the past (20–30) and will be able to determine if that number drops by 50 percent.

5.4	Changing Process Goals to Results Goals

Process Goal ➡	Why do we want to do this?	➡ **Results Goal**
Describes means *We will integrate an integrated math/science curriculum.*	So that . . .	**Describes ends** *Freshman failure rate is reduced.*
Describes inputs *We will hire star-quality teachers.*	So that . . .	**Describes outputs** *Student achievement improves.*
Aims at capacity improvements *We will budget additional time for staff collaboration.*	So that . . .	**Aims productivity improvements** *Staff are more focused on improving student results.*
Involves system interventions *We will implement block scheduling.*	So that . . .	**Involves projected outcomes** *Students have deeper understanding of the material.*
Focuses on improvement activities *We will develop a districtwide writing rubric.*	So that . . .	**Identifies improvement targets** *Students' writing improves.*

• *Attainable.* Current data confirms that this goal is neither so conservative to be uninspiring nor so high that people will think it's impossible to achieve.

• *Results-oriented.* The goal describes the desired outcome ("reduce the number of students needing assistance"), not the process or activity that *might* contribute to attaining this outcome.

• *Timebound.* The goal sets a deadline for accomplishment ("within the next two years").

To be truly useful measurement tools, goals should specify improvement targets that define the performance level we would like to see. They should address the specific indicators we will look for as evidence of progress. We should also have in mind the specific tools (tests and other measures) we will use to monitor progress on each goal. Not only are SMART goals inspirational (and "worthy of commitment"), they are eminently *practical*—data-based and reflective of what we believe is possible, given current performance.

In his book *Results: The Key to Continuous School Improvement,* Mike Schmoker reminds us of the cost of basing improvement efforts on goals that are not measured against results:

> Emphasizing only one major or untested process, without careful and frequent analysis, can be disastrous. An example is when the New York City schools poured $120 million into a single process, guidance services, which had never been tested against results. Four years later, schools found that the process did not affect their goal—to reduce the dropout rate (Schmoker, 1998, p. 4).

This is only one example of how we educators can sometimes be our own worst enemies when it comes to reform. On the one hand, we are eager to constantly improve the educational process, so we make

changes in our schools and classrooms. But after we make improvement-minded changes, we often neglect to measure them against any benchmark of improved student learning. Without measures, we can't demonstrate any improvement, so we move on to the next change. No wonder the public accuses us of following fads and gurus!

Over time, in districts and schools that persist in implementing process goals without specific results, people lose faith that new approaches will have any positive impact on the current situation. Many educators grow to resist and resent efforts at change, and it becomes that much more difficult for true innovations and "best practices" to take root.

SMART goals offer a way out of this trap. When we focus our collaborative efforts on data-based, student-centered SMART goals and build-in time to reflect on student progress against those goals, we grow our sense of success and professional efficacy. And each time we reflect on the results, we create more momentum for self-initiated change and improvement.

SMART Goals by "Altitude"

We noted in Chapter 2 that *focus* is a matter of "altitude." The SMART goals that define focus also vary by the system level where they're created: district, school, or classroom. As shown in Figure 5.5, at each level, SMART goals address vision, mission, values, beliefs, and priorities; together, these elements are the elastic that binds the goals together and ensures we are focusing improvement on high-leverage areas. However, depending on altitude, SMART goals serve different purposes and are derived and monitored differently.

At the district level, SMART goals aim at *groups* of students and are identified by

| 5.5 | **Goals and "Altitude"** |

Vision, Mission, Values, Beliefs, Priorities

District Level

Academic Indicators
Benchmarks. Measured by standardized/state/aptitude tests.

Climate Indicators
Perceptions. Measured by school-based surveys in all schools.

Behavior Indicators
Expectations. Measured by behavioral data (attendance, suspensions, graduation rate, etc.).

Growth measured annually, over time, by demographics.

School Level

Academic Indicators
Content/performance standards. Measured by standardized/state/aptitude tests, district tests, criterion-referenced GPA.

Climate Indicators
Perceptions of stakeholders at our school. Measured by school-based surveys, interviews, and focus groups.

Behavior Indicators
Expectations. Measured by behavioral data (attendance, behavior referrals, etc.).

Growth measured annually, pre-post, over time, by demographics.

Classroom Level

Academic Indicators
Skills, competencies, performances. Measured by pre-post district and school-based tests, ongoing classroom assessments (common measures), criterion-referenced GPA.

Climate Indicators
Perceptions of students and families in our classrooms. Measured by classroom-developed surveys, interviews, and focus groups.

Behavior Indicators
Expectations. Measured by behavioral data (study skills, engagement in learning, independence, cooperative learning, etc.)

Growth measured daily, weekly, monthly, etc. Measurement is ongoing.

examining patterns and trends over time. Their purpose is to provide inspiration, challenge, and direction, and for this reason, district-level goals are broadly stated and aimed at significant "gateways" or benchmarks of student learning. (For example, many districts identify the ability to read at grade level by the end of 3rd grade a SMART goal.) District-level SMART goals are monitored annually over time and by demographic differences (hence the use of standardized and district assessments). The time line to achieve a district-level SMART goal, inasmuch as these goals are part of the district's strategic plan, is usually at least five years.

At the school level, SMART goals provide direction to the work of the school. Like district-level goals, school-level SMART goals aim at *groups* of students and are identified by examining patterns and trends over time. However, school-level goals are often more specific than district goals; they are driven by content and/or performance standards and are based on the needs of the students at that particular school. Again, like district SMART goals, school SMART goals are measured annually and over time; standardized and district-developed assessments are used to monitor the progress of the school as a whole. Ideally staff and administration are asking not only, "How many of our students achieved at specified levels?" but also, "Did our students grow at least one academic year's worth of learning?" Many of the useful school SMART goals we have seen have been written as annual improvement goals; others have been worked in to longer-term (usually three-year) strategic improvement plans.

At the classroom level, (or the subject area/department level), SMART goals provide a laser-like focus to the collaborative work of teaching and learning. They aim at both *groups* of students and *individual* students and are identified by looking at *this year's* students. Classroom SMART goals are often written more in the language of curriculum objectives and particular skill sets and competencies. They are measured more frequently (weekly or monthly), through diagnostic-based, periodic, and ongoing assessment tools. The operative questions are, "Are our students growing at an adequate

(or better) rate of progress?" and "What instructional strategies and programming work best for which students?" Classroom-level SMART goals allow teachers to (1) more rapidly identify those students who need help, (2) challenge the students in the middle to reach a little bit higher, and (3) move students who have mastered the material on to new skills and competencies. The shorter time lines give teachers the kind of quick feedback needed to make the continuous adjustments to instructional strategies and programming necessary to enhance student learning—ideally, long before the end of the school year.

The following sections provide a more detailed discussion of SMART goals at the district, school, and classroom levels and provide guidelines for developing and using SMART goals at each altitude.

District SMART Goals

To make progress across an entire school district, the district as a whole needs to be focused on a select number of goals that are broadly-stated but still clear and results-oriented. At the district level, SMART goals should provide vision, focus, direction, and support for the schools and their more specific goals. Here are some questions that can help districts identify the "vital few" priority goals:

• "Where are our students strongest in their skills and knowledge? On what measures?"

• "Where are our students weakest?"

• "Looking at our student results over time, what can we say about where our system's strengths and "gaps" are in curriculum, instruction, and staff development?"

• "What other indicators of a healthy system are important to us? (These might include attendance rates, college acceptance, and parent/staff/student satisfaction.) How is our school doing on those indicators? Which of these indicators should we focus on that will have the greatest positive impact for our students?"

Here is a sampling of district-level goals:

• "All students will be reading at grade level by the end of 3rd grade."

• "All students will demonstrate proficiency in all tested areas (reading, language arts, math, science, and social studies) by the time they graduate."

• "The district will rank in the state's academic top 10."

• "The number of 8th, 10th, and 12th grade students reported as being drug- and alcohol-free will increase in comparison to baseline data."

• "All 9th graders will successfully complete Algebra, and all 10th graders will successfully complete Geometry."

Notice that these goals do not include prescribed processes or any specific targets and time lines that might encroach on individual schools' ability to achieve these outcomes through their own more specific SMART goals. At the district level, SMART goals should only identify important *large-scale indicators* (defining, for example, what the district means by "improved student achievement," or "a safer, more respectful learning environment") and trustworthy *measures*. Figure 5.6 shows how these two pieces fit together.

Once district SMART goals are set and the goals' indicators and measures are in place, it will be up to individual action teams or site-based school improvement teams to determine more specific targets and time lines, based on their data and their capacity for change. Establishing SMART goals at the district level provides

5.6	Indicators and Measures for District-Level Goals	
District Goal	**Indicators**	**Measures**
"Improved student achievement."	1. Increased numbers of students reading by 3rd grade 2. Increased number of students able to pass algebra and geometry 3. Number of students exiting from tutoring/special services 4. Percent of students taking and passing AP tests	1. District-developed rubric or 3rd grade standardized reading test 2. GPA for these courses 3. Special services enrollment log 4. AP test
"A safer, more respectful learning environment."	1. Increased parent, student, and staff satisfaction with school climate 2. Decreased suspensions, expulsions 3. Attendance and truancy rates	1. Climate surveys 2. Behavioral reports by school 3. Attendance reports by school

Copyright © 2001 by Quality Leadership by Design, LLC. Reprinted with permission.

focused energy and momentum to strategic systemwide improvement.

School SMART Goals

To set SMART goals at the school level, the principals, teachers, staff, parents, and students need to ask broad questions about their particular student population. The following questions are good starting points:

• "In which areas of the standardized tests were students weakest this year—math, reading, language arts, science, social studies? Has this been a consistently weak area for all students or just for this particular group of students?"

• "What patterns do we see in the standardized test data? Who is in the top 25 percent? Middle 50 percent? How are girls doing compared to boys? Children of color compared to Caucasian children? Is mobility a factor? Attendance? Motivation? How is our special education population doing? How is our English language learner population doing?"

• "What programs, curricula, and instructional strategies have our top, middle, and low achieving students been exposed to? Do we see any patterns or trends?"

• "Are there other performance measures that verify our school's weaknesses in particular areas? Do we have district or classroom assessments to back this up?"

• "Which aspects of school climate are most important to our students, families and staff? How is each group of stakeholders perceiving our school? Are there demographic differences?"

• "Which of the most important aspects are most strongly related to student learning? On which are we weakest?"

We recommend schools set just one or two SMART goals focused on learning improvement and no more than one SMART goal focused on "climate" (which might address an issue such as safety or respect). Individual grade, subject area, or department teams can then develop their own goals, based on their particular student needs. Pareto analysis, discussed in Chapters 2 and 3 and illustrated in Figure 5.7, provides one way for schools to examine areas of need and identify the most important issues.

Within the SMART goal setting process, Pareto thinking helps educators identify manageable pieces of big problems and pinpoint where improvement efforts are likely to have the greatest effect. How "far down" you have to delve varies by situation. The teachers who developed the Pareto shown in Figure 5.7 needed to go down three levels of thinking before they felt they had a sufficiently narrow scope for writing a useful SMART goal. Once they had determined which comprehension skill *most* needed improvement ("drawing conclusions"), they began to emphasize instructional strategies that gave students ample practice with this skill. These strategies involved using a variety of materials, assigning student teams to present their own lessons about how to draw conclusions, and structuring oral exercises in drawing conclusions prior to reading activities.

To be realistic, SMART goals at the school level should extend out no more than three years. Schools also need to think about results-oriented goals, indicators, measures, and specific targets. When establishing targets, the school should look at its data and ask the following questions:

• "What is the baseline?"

• "How aggressive are we prepared to be? Over what time period?"

• "How will other parts of our program be affected? How might other parts of the system be affected?"

5.7 | **SMART Goal Targeting Through Pareto Analysis**

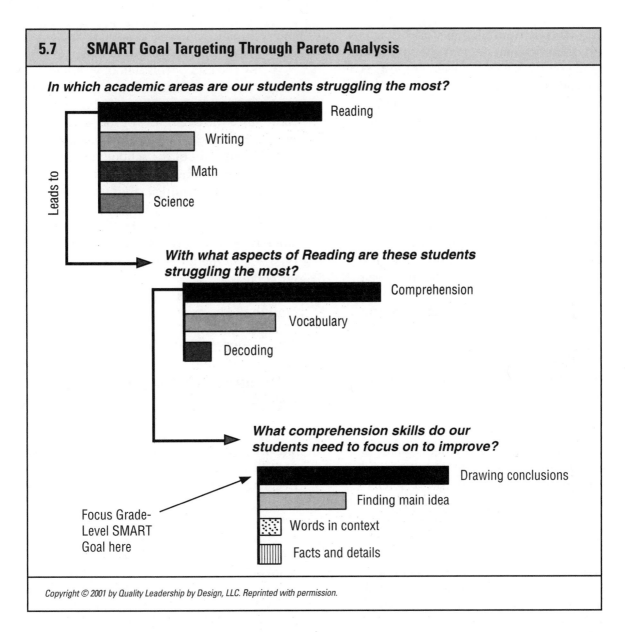

In which academic areas are our students struggling the most?

Reading
Writing
Math
Science

Leads to

With what aspects of Reading are these students struggling the most?

Comprehension
Vocabulary
Decoding

What comprehension skills do our students need to focus on to improve?

Drawing conclusions
Finding main idea
Words in context
Facts and details

Focus Grade-Level SMART Goal here

• "What might be the intended and unintended consequences of pursuing this target?"

Classroom and Subject Area SMART Goals

Districts and schools have the luxury of looking out several years to set desired goals. In contrast, classroom teachers need SMART goals that will help them get feedback quickly. They are interested in improving their instructional practice *now*, so that they can help this year's students as well as future ones.

At the classroom level, it's tempting to try to build SMART goals around standardized test results; for example: "Increase by

15 percent the number of students achieving acceptable mastery on the state's 5th grade mathematics achievement test." We strongly recommend limiting the number of SMART goals directly tied to standardized test results. Although these scores are an important end-of-the-year data point, they are also a lot like morbidity rates hospitals publish: They can tell you how many failures occurred, but too late in the process to do anything about it. Many teachers do not see classroom breakdowns of their students' individual standardized test results until the school year is almost over (if they see these results at all). If you must wait until the last month of school to find that students haven't made the gains you've hoped for, there's precious little time to remedy the situation!

In addition, using standardized tests as the only measure of student learning puts teachers in danger of providing narrow instruction—of "teaching to the tests"—rather than thinking about the whole teaching-learning experience. Finally, if standardized tests are the only measure, then how does an art, music, or foreign language teacher learn how to examine and improve his or her practice? How can social workers, psychologists, and other key support staff improve the behavioral processes that affect student learning experiences?

There are a variety of assessment tools available to teachers that allow them to measure student progress throughout the year. Note the diversity of measures associated with the following classroom and subject-specific SMART goals:

• "By the end of the semester, achieve a 20-percent increase in the number of students at *Level 23 reading*."

• "By the end of the school year, increase by 10 percent the number of 1st and 2nd graders who can aurally identify musical instruments, as measured by *the textbook's pretests and post-tests*."

• "By the end of this school year, increase student attendance by 50 percent for students who have been absent 7 days or more since the beginning of the school year, *as measured by daily attendance logs*."

• "By the end of the school year, improve students' phonemic awareness to an average of 90 percent *on a dictated-sentence assessment*."

• "By the end of the school year, female students will achieve a score of 3 or higher on a *4-point rubric measuring strength performance*."

• "By the end of this year, 85 percent of our 9th grade students will score either proficient or advanced on the *district-developed writing rubric*."

A Process Tool for Developing SMART Goals

The process for developing a goal that's SMART involves thinking through a variety of indicators, measures, and targets. The tree diagram, illustrated in Figure 5.8, provides a very useful tool for school, department, or classroom-level goal-setting teams. We believe the real power in using a tree diagram lies in applying it as a "structured brainstorming" tool. It helps groups to be creative and think outside standard answers, but it is also structured enough to help outline the group's thinking and keep everyone focused on what's important: creating a yearly, quarterly, or more frequently measured SMART goal.

With Figure 5.8 serving as a reference, let's go through the steps of using a tree diagram to help develop an academic SMART goal.

1. **Choose a results-oriented goal**. This could be a schoolwide goal or a

5.8 | Tree Diagram Template

Indicators

Standards and objectives (weak areas for students).

Measures

Tools we'll use to determine where students are now and whether they are improving.

Targets

The attainable performance level we'd like to see.

SMART Goals

Specific and strategic, measurable, attainable, results-oriented, and timebound.

Results-Oriented Goal

Ultimate improvement we want to see in students' skills, competencies, performance.

Indicator #1	Measure #1.1	Target #1.1
	Measure #1.2	Target #1.2
Indicator #2	Measure #2.1	Target #2.1
	Measure #2.2	Target #2.2
	Measure #2.3	Target #2.3
Indicator #3	Measure #3.1	Target #3.1

5.9	Indicator Examples	
Goal		**Indicators**
"Improve reading skills."		Increased vocabulary Recognizing main idea Drawing conclusions Making inferences Decoding new words
"Improve analytical thinking skills."		Complex problem solving Gathering information Organizing information Generating ideas Synthesizing elements Evaluating outcomes
"Improve school climate."		Increased trust between families/students and school Reduced number of threats/harassment Increased number of families/students at school events More students involved in co-curriculars

grade-, department-, or subject-level goal. Be sure to consider content and performance standards and how students perform against those standards. Here are some examples:

• "Improve reading skills of 3rd grade students."

• "Improve the critical thinking skills of 6th, 7th, and 8th grade students."

• "Improve students' analytical thinking skills and problem solving methods in grades 9–12."

When you've selected a results-oriented goal, write it in the far-left box of a form set up like Figure 5.8.

2. **Develop indicators for the goal.** Indicators are the evidence we look for to see if goals are being achieved. For achievement/learning goals, indicators describe those skills and performances that are aligned with standards, benchmarks, and learner objectives. Kick off your brainstorming of goal indications with this question: "What would *good* _____ (goal area) look like?" For example, if your goal were to improve writing, you would ask, "What would *good writing* look like?" You might reply, "complete sentences," "has a logical flow," "correct use of punctuation," and so on. (See Figure 5.9 for additional examples of indicators.) After assembling a list of "good features," use a focusing question to select only the "vital few" skill areas. Then ask, "Which of these skills do our students most need to improve and *how* do we know these are the skills most in need of improvement?" When possible, we

recommend using data to determine the answer to this question; if there are no data available, use your intuitive judgment. With or without data, your indicators should be limited to only those skills areas that students really need to work on.

3. **Identify measures for the indicators.** Let's say one of your goals is to improve students' reading skills, and you have identified "increased vocabulary" as an indicator of improved reading. But you still don't have enough information to help you study and improve your ability to improve students' reading skills. What's missing is how you're going to *measure* "improved vocabulary." You need to define, in very practical terms, how you will assign a number or score to this indicator. Whether you're using the tree diagram in a group or by yourself, be sure to consider both annual standardized measures and ongoing measures that are classroom or district based. As the sample tree diagram in Figure 5.8 shows, you might be able to monitor student progress on some indicators with just one measure; others indicators will require more.

If possible, when developing schoolwide SMART goals and classroom/subject area goals, have teachers from the same grade level or subject talk about measures they currently use to evaluate student progress. Teachers often find they can use their time more effectively if they agree on standard versions of quizzes, tests, and other classroom-based assessments. This allows them to review students' progress across classrooms and pool ideas for improvement.

4. **Develop targets for improvement.** Carefully review any available data on your students' current level of performance, and identify a reasonable target for improvement on every measure. If no data are available (which may be the case because often new measures must be developed), we recommend picking a "ceiling number"—just look up at the ceiling and pick the first number that pops into your head. Any number is better than no number; at least it's something to shoot for. Similarly, if you have data but don't have a feel for what kind of improvement is possible because you haven't yet gone through the process of setting goals, implementing strategies, monitoring progress, and making adjustments, it's difficult to know what target to set. A general rule of thumb: The more experience you have with your data, the more specific your targets can be. In either of these cases, even if student achievement falls short of your inexact target you will still have something to measure results against and a baseline for monitoring improvement.

5. **Select one or two goals to work on.** With specific indicators, measures, and targets outlined, your group should be able to identify a few SMART goals you want to pursue for the year, the semester, or some other designated time frame. Write each SMART goal on its own line, at the far right of the tree diagram template. Remember: It isn't necessary—or even desirable—to have a lot of goals; better to have one or two goals that focus on your *vital few* improvement issues.

Appendix A provides additional examples of tree diagrams for academic SMART goals at elementary, middle, and high school levels and a tree diagram for a SMART goal focused on school climate.

Data's Role in SMART Goal Setting

The "A" in the SMART acronym—"attainable"—is a hallmark that cannot be overlooked. At every level, whether district, school, or classroom, you must do all you can to ensure the targets you've set are realistic. Data are the key.

For example, in a district where school planning councils comprise teachers, administrators, and parents, a middle school group came up with the following one-year SMART school goal: "By May of next year, 85 percent of our 6th, 7th, and 8th graders will be at the proficient or advanced level on the district writing assessment." Unfortunately, the group set this goal without having carefully examined the data on students' current writing performance.

When the school council went back to the data (shown in Figure 5.10) they realized this goal might not be attainable. Even in the best performing set—6th grade—only 36 percent of the students were at the proficient and advanced levels. And the other grades were performing much worse!

It was clear to the school council that raising all rates to 85 percent in just one year would be extremely difficult unless the students worked on nothing but writing all year long (*distorting the system*), or teachers devoted time to developing a breakthrough technique for teaching writing skills (fundamentally *changing the system*). The school was unwilling to make either commitment, so the council decided on a more attainable

one-year goal: "By May of next year, 20 percent of all 6th, 7th, and 8th grade students at the minimal, basic, and proficient levels will improve to the next level of writing ability as measured by the district writing assessment."

Working on SMART goals allowed this school to make a highly strategic decision to pursue an incremental improvement rather than a "breakthrough improvement." It has decided to set up quarterly monitoring of both student-writing results and the processes teachers and students use to get those results. Based on what staff members learn, the school council will set a new improvement goal and new plans for next year.

The McFarland School District went through a similar process. The "school improvement teams" from the district's five sites developed SMART academic goals and climate goals. After examining the data shown in Figure 5.11, the team from McFarland Elementary School generated the following SMART climate goal: "By the end of this school year, the number of behavioral referrals to the principal in the areas of fighting and threatening/harassment will decrease by 20 percent."

The McFarland Elementary team settled on this SMART goal because fighting and harassment were the top two reasons for referrals, and a 20-percent reduction would

5.10	Middle School's Writing Proficiencies				
Incoming Students	**Minimum**	**Basic**	**Proficient**	**Advanced**
6th graders	14%	50%	33%	3%
7th graders	24%	60%	13%	1%
8th graders	27%	45%	28%	-0-

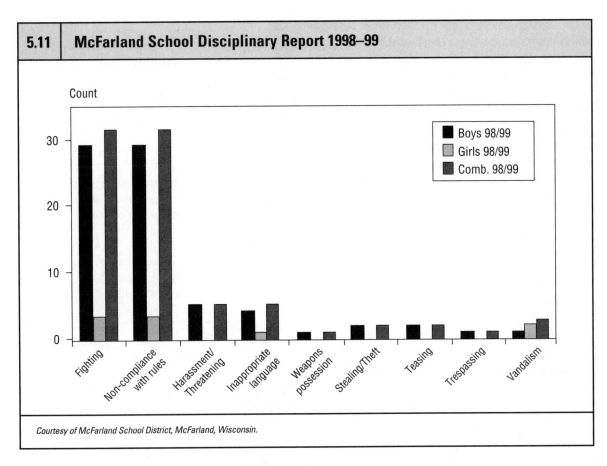

| 5.11 | **McFarland School Disciplinary Report 1998–99** |

Count

Legend: Boys 98/99, Girls 98/99, Comb. 98/99

Courtesy of McFarland School District, McFarland, Wisconsin.

work out to approximately 15 fewer student referrals—a number the team felt was attainable. Team members were familiar with the Pareto principle and understood that if they focused their improvement efforts on the "vital few" problems, they would come to understand the nature of those problems so well that the improvement strategies they eventually put in place would most likely alleviate the "important other" problems as well.

Here are a few more examples of data-based, realistic schoolwide SMART academic goals:

• "Improve to 90 percent in the next three years the percentage of students reading proficiently as measured by the reading subtest of the 4th grade state administered criterion-referenced test" (current proficiency is 70 percent).

• "In the next two years, increase to 85 percent the number of incoming 9th graders able to successfully complete Algebra" (current success rate is 75 percent).

• "Over an instructional year, achieve 100 percent of students in targeted classrooms who demonstrate one year's growth in applying analytical thinking skills as indicated on performance assessments."

Integrating School and District Goals

In an aligned system, classroom and school goals drive the goals being set systemwide because the data "bubble up" from the teachers, based on their work with students. For example, schools in the Whitewater Unified School District follow a cyclical improvement process, with regular activities scheduled throughout the year. As illustrated in Figure 5.12, each summer, Whitewater's schools establish goals based on an assessment of students' learning needs; then they develop school improvement plans, which they bring to the school board for strategic alignment. The board uses these plans as the basis for its annual budget. The next year, Whitewater's schools develop new goals, based on a reassessment of students' needs, and the planning-budgeting cycle continues.

In the Verona Area School District, each individual school has the power to set goals and to assign budget resources (the schools control over 80 percent of the district's budget, including funds for staffing, curriculum, and staff development). Each of Verona's schools presents the board with an "Operating Plan," which includes the school's action plans and budget allocations for accomplishing goals. In this "bottom-up" process, the board's role is to ensure that the district's priorities and resources support the schools' goals and then help remove barriers (such as district policies and procedures) that might impede schools' progress. As evidenced by Verona's reputation for academic excellence and innovative programming, when schools have this kind of control over the resources necessary to pursue their goals, the increased efficiencies result in rapid, ongoing improvement.

5.12	A Calendar for Improving Student Achievement

June – August
Site teams analyze data and plan for improvement

August – September
Site teams establish improvement plans based on identified district priorities and site needs
Plans specify targets for improvement

October
Site teams present improvement plans outlines to the board at a public meeting
The board provides input regarding plans and targets

October – May
Site teams implement improvement plans and gather assessment data

December
Budget priorities are set knowing current focus of improvement

March
Budget recommendations presented

June
Site teams report results to the board at a public meeting; provide initial analysis of assessment data
The board provides input regarding results and implemented plan

June – June (12-month period)
Process repeats

Courtesy of Whitewater Unified School District, Whitewater, Wisconsin.

Developing Robust Improvement Activities

Setting a SMART goal is a beginning. The next step is to use sound staff development practices to start planning instructional and programmatic improvements that will support teachers' efforts to help students learn. We usually recommend that school staffs begin by reviewing what they already know about best practices in the goal area. This may require some brainstorming and research. Next, teachers should identify any best practices they are already incorporating and would like to know more about. According to Sue Abplanalp, principal of Lowell Elementary School, teachers should be given the opportunity to identify *how* they want to learn. Sue provides her faculty with a matrix checklist listing the following staff development options:

- Attend an onsite workshop.
- Attend an offsite workshop. (Upon return, teachers are expected to provide inservice training for colleagues.)
- Observe or mentor another teacher.
- Work with a peer.
- Establish a study group.
- Use video-based instruction.

Once a school has selected a staff development approach (or approaches), teachers should participate in an ongoing, collaborative, specifically focused manner (see King & Newmann, 2000) so that their learning is truly connected to—and will help achieve—the identified SMART goal. When teachers feel they have a new level of understanding about the goal area, they can work together to identify the precise instructional strategies or programmatic changes they want to implement. We recommend the following four-step process as a way to select strategies/approaches for implementation:

1. List as many improvement activities as possible. Make sure they relate directly to the SMART goal.

2. Evaluate the listed activities and eliminate unreasonable and/or powerless ones.

3. Rank the remaining activities by importance. (Consider using multi-voting.)

4. Select only those activities that can be accomplished within the given time frame and with the available resources.

As teachers gain confidence with the new improvement strategies, they should continue to plan and talk together about how they will incorporate those strategies into department and school practice and how they will support and encourage each other on an ongoing basis.

The Wisconsin Heights School District makes a strong case for linking teachers' professional development plans to school and district goals. Wisconsin Heights teachers can access written copies of school and district goals via a "drop-down menu" available on classroom computers. This easy access to higher-altitude goals helps them develop individual professional development plans that will support district and school goals achievement. (See Appendix B for an example professional development plan.) The resulting goal alignment has prompted some interesting changes at each of the district's four schools, all of which are at the early stages of continuous improvement.

- At the high school, teachers began tuning in much more closely to their building goals. One teacher commented that at first, he had resented having to work on a schoolwide goal. Later on, having considered the goal around school culture and climate, he asked for assistance structuring a professional development goal, saying, "I need to focus on why we're having problems and what I can do about them."

- At the middle school, teachers have taken the schoolwide SMART goals to heart such that they've laminated a list of the goals and have posted a copy in every classroom—including the gymnasium and the art and music classrooms.

- At the elementary schools, many teachers are incorporating SMART goals into their professional development plans.

A "SMART" Process for Improvement

The positive changes within the Wisconsin Heights district are the result of an intensive amount of professional staff development. And the *way* development is being implemented has as much to do with the changes as the specific focus of the development. Wisconsin Heights has taken a results-oriented, job-embedded approach.

Our own commitment to best practices in professional development led us to look for a job-and-improvement-embedded development approach we could use with our clients within the SMART goals process. We were thus inspired when we discovered Mike Schmoker's (1996) "33 minute meeting agenda," which provides structure for teams of teachers interested in using student data to help achieve group goals. We have expanded this notion into a series of "30+ Minute Meetings," detailed in Figure 5.13.

Many of the schools, departments, and grade-level teams we work with are finding this structured process to be a very effective way of building professional competency and improving student learning. Each meeting capitalizes on the power of combining a *focused* agenda with data-based *reflection* and *collaborative* skills to drive improvement of student results. Briefly, the 30+ Minute Meeting Series breaks down like this:

- **First meeting:** The group identifies a student learning need. *Between the first and second meeting:* A study team gathers data to verify the need.
- **Second meeting:** The group develops SMART goals. *Between the second and third meeting:* Study teams review literature and best practice research about the student learning area.
- **Third meeting:** The group identifies what members are already doing that is best

practice and determines further staff development needs. *Between the third and fourth meetings:* A study team investigates staff development delivery alternatives (Figure 4.3's checklist of staff development options on page 74 provides a good starting point).

- **Fourth meeting:** The group discusses the methods, and individuals identify their preferred mode for learning new "best practices." *Between the fourth and fifth meetings:* Implement staff development activities. Implement "best practices" in classrooms and monitor results.
- **Fifth meeting:** The group reflects on the data and decides the next steps.

Learning from SMART Goals

Developing SMART goals is not a one-time event. Regular monitoring of students' progress toward these goals allows educators to adjust instructional strategies and professional development activities against intended results. When we develop SMART goals, then align our curriculum, programs, and instructional practices to achieve those goals, the result is improvements to our own systems of teaching and learning that ultimately promote student learning and achievement.

In other words, creating shared responsibility is a dynamic learning process, and it revolves around schools' ability to use inquiry and reflection to achieve meaningful goals. When teachers are using SMART goals to learn, they

- Set specific, measurable, learner-focused goals together.
- Plan how to help learners accomplish these goals.
- Gather evidence of individual and class progress toward the goal.
- Share their results.

5.13	**The 30+ Minute Meeting Series**

These meetings can be conducted as a whole staff, by grade-level teams, or by departments.

Meeting 1. Identify and isolate the opportunity or "gap" between what is wanted and the current situation.
5 min.   The presenting question: What are the student learning issues we are struggling with?
10 min.   Brainstorm responses.
5 min.   Identify top three priorities by multi-voting.
10 min.   What more do we need to know? How can we find out?
Between meetings—Gather student data/information on priority areas.

Meeting 2. Identify SMART Goal(s) for priority areas.
10 min.   Present graphs of student performance in areas of concern. (Focus on skill areas or proficiency/ performance levels.)
10 min.   Brainstorm results-oriented goals for priority areas.
5 min.   Select one results-oriented goal for each priority area.
10 min.   Make the results goals SMART: Individuals write indicators, measures, and targets for each goal. (Consider *indicators* by skill/competence/performance expectations aligned to standards; consider both standardized and classroom-based *measures*; consider student data when writing *targets*.)
5 min.   Share SMART goals round-robin, one at a time.
15 min.   Group selects "best of" indicators, measures, and targets to write group SMART goal.
10 min.   What do we need to know to affect student learning for this SMART goal?
Between meetings—Conduct literature/research/best practice reviews.

Meeting 3. Correlate best practices to current practices.
10 min.   Share information gathered between meetings.
10 min.   Matrix: What are we already doing that supports best practice in this area? What more would we like to learn about?
10 min.   Identify instructional strategies we want to do more of, start doing, and stop doing.
Between meetings—Research ways we can develop our professional knowledge to learn best practices.

Meeting 4. Identify preferred staff development methods.
10 min.   Share information about various staff development methods.
10 min.   Matrix: Individuals select preferred strategy for learning about best practices and identify areas in which they are willing to coach/teach others.
15 min.   Discuss implementation. How will we implement staff development for best practices? What support do we need? How will we measure progress on the SMART goal?
Between meetings—Implement staff development and best practices integration. Gather data to measure against the baseline.

Meeting 5. Analyze the results and refocus.
10 min.   Present graphs of new data.
15 min.   Discuss what worked, what didn't, and why.
15 min.   If the instructional strategy worked well, discuss how to "hold the gains." If the strategy did not work well, decide the next steps: Start doing the strategy differently? Stop doing the strategy altogether? Start a new strategy?
Start the cycle over again.

| 5.14 | **The SMART PDSA Learning Wheel** |

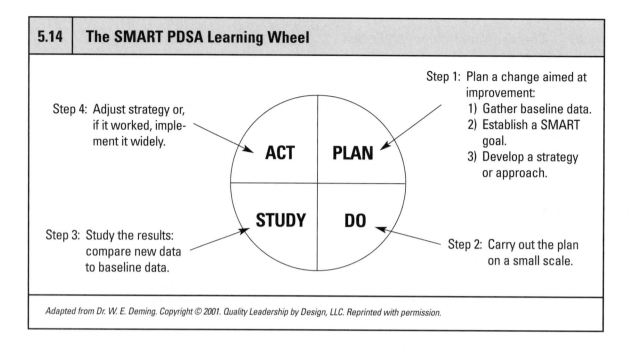

Step 4: Adjust strategy or, if it worked, implement it widely.

ACT   **PLAN**

STUDY   **DO**

Step 1: Plan a change aimed at improvement:
1) Gather baseline data.
2) Establish a SMART goal.
3) Develop a strategy or approach.

Step 3: Study the results: compare new data to baseline data.

Step 2: Carry out the plan on a small scale.

Adapted from Dr. W. E. Deming. Copyright © 2001. Quality Leadership by Design, LLC. Reprinted with permission.

• Adjust teaching strategies based on what they're learning together.

• Develop new plans for meeting their goals.

This sequence delineates a powerful learning cycle, called "PDSA" for *"Plan–Do–Study–Act."*

PDSA was first taught by W. Edwards Deming in the 1940s. (Science teachers will quickly recognize it as the scientific method). There are four steps in the PSDA learning cycle: (1) *plan* a strategy or change; (2) *do* it—on a small scale at first; (3) *study* the results using data and other forms of feedback; and (4) *act*—either implement the plan full-scale or revise both the plan and its implementation. As Figure 5.14 shows, we have adapted the PDSA learning cycle to include SMART goals at the front end as a way to communicate the continuous, never-ending nature of goal setting. Each "turn" of this "learning wheel" informs the next level of improvement and builds a

stronger learning community that understands what works, what doesn't, and why.

From a teacher's perspective, this method—setting SMART goals up front, then "turning the wheel" to learn as rapidly as possible—makes a lot of sense. After all, most teachers have only 9 to 10 months with students and can't afford to waste time on ineffective strategies. To keep student learning on course, feedback on the effectiveness of instruction, curriculum, and programs must be rapid and regular.

There are multiple possible forums for sharing teacher learning, from small team sessions to large groups where everyone is encouraged to reflect on what they have learned and to determine how to apply the new knowledge within their own practice. Questions such as, "How did you do that?" "What were your results? How do you know?" and "What would you do differently next time?" are part of an open dialogue. In this manner, schools can create an environment where learning is experienced as a process of "failing forward"—learning from one's successes as well as from one's mistakes. In this type of environment, change doesn't happen for the sake of change; it happens because it's an improvement. In these schools, leadership is a process of ongoing, shared learning.

When individuals within the system develop targets and time lines *themselves,* and *for themselves,* they add a positive challenge and degree of specificity that can help them focus their time and resources. When targets and time lines are reviewed as part of a natural learning cycle, they help the whole system focus on improvement.

Summary: SMART Goals

SMART goals—goals that are specific and strategic, measurable, attainable, results-oriented, and timebound—are a tool that educators can use to turn desires into results. They help us develop practical steps toward improvement that combine the three elements of the framework for shared responsibility (focus, reflection, and collaboration).

The nature of SMART goals varies, depending on whether they are developed and applied in the classroom, at the school level, or districtwide. In a school or a district that embraces continuous improvement and is committed to building capacity as a way to meet its goals, the processes outlined in this chapter can help teachers learn from both their success meeting goals and their experiences of "failing forward." As a high school principal framed it, "Goals aren't destinations. They're just the next place to stop and see what's next."

6 Leadership

Always keep Ithaca fixed in your mind,
to arrive there is your ultimate goal.
But do not hurry the voyage at all.
It is better to let it last for long years;
And even to anchor at the isle when you are old,
Rich with all that you have gained on the way,
not expecting that Ithaca will offer you riches.

—CAVAFY, THE POET OF ALEXANDRIA FROM "THE JOURNEY TO ITHACA"

It's August 21, the first day back for teachers in the Hartland/Lakeside School District after an especially busy summer of curriculum work and staff development. The air is charged with the usual energy and excitement a new school year brings. As the district's teachers and principals wait for an all-staff meeting to begin, they reconnect with each other, meet new staff members, and busily exchange stories about all the work that's left to do before the students arrive.

Superintendent Jeff Gruber gently brings the group to order so the program can begin on time. After a warm welcome back and a few logistic reminders, Dr. Gruber invites a panel of teachers and principals up to the front of the auditorium and introduces them to the assembly[*]:

> These people have been working all summer, attending data workshops and developing their skills as leaders. They will be working throughout the year with all the staff to share what they learned this summer and to help us, as a whole system, continue to improve the results we achieve with our students. They represent what I believe is a hallmark of our district. For several years now, through the work of our Continuing Quality Improvement Council, department chair meetings, and ongoing staff development, we have been building momentum toward a vision of leadership to which each and every one of us can aspire. And that's only going to mean better

---

[*]Remarks by Jeff Gruber and Wendy Lombard come from an unpublished transcript of the Hartland/Lakeside District staff meeting held August 21, 2000.

things for the children and families we serve. I've asked each of them to share a few words with you about what their experiences this summer have meant to them.

One-by-one, the panelists step to the microphone and speak, some from prepared notes, some from memory, and all from the heart. The final comments come from 6th grade teacher Wendy Lombard. "I was pretty nervous about doing this," she admits to her colleagues, "so I thought I better prepare something in advance. I'll just read it to you if you don't mind." Wendy looks down at her statement and begins to read:

> I feel that there is really a vision within and for our school district taking shape and becoming more clearly defined day by day. It is a vision that involves constant forward movement toward goals of excellence in education. One of the best things about this feeling I have is I really believe the administrative leadership wants the plan for moving forward to come from those of us who work with the kids.
>
> I have worked on many committees, attended many meetings, and participated in many seminars since I began teaching in this school district. I've been here for 22 years and this is the first time I have felt that there is truly a desire to move toward a goal of excellence; there is a vision that still needs clarification and refinement from everyone in this district who wants to contribute; and the plan is really *not* already decided.
>
> In fact, the plan for how to improve and grow as a district depends on those of us who want to participate in its development. This is the first time in all these years I have felt empowered in this way— not that I think I or any one of us has power and control, but that each of us can make significant contributions to the positive growth of this school district *if we choose to do so.* No one committee, no certain cluster of "chosen ones" are predestined to make big decisions alone.

> As I participated in the data and leadership seminars, I had to keep reminding myself, as we discussed and analyzed different information and concepts, that I had to think beyond my classroom. As a teacher, I approach every seminar, every workshop with, "What can I get out of this to immediately use with my kids?" I realized that if I was willing to slow down my pace and listen in terms of *district improvement* as well as *self-improvement,* I would gain better insight into what we hope to move toward. There is a vision that involves forward movement toward excellence, but the vision is not entirely clear until we all help to shape it. I really feel that is not only what is *needed,* but what is *desired* by our administration.
>
> We will all begin this school year with some expectations. Some are positive and some are negative. Already some of us are unhappy about situations at our schools that involve us personally, and justifiably unhappy, most likely. Hopefully in the spirit of improving our district's efforts to do what is best for our kids, teachers and administrators will be able to work out our differences. I think we are really at a point where we have a fresh, new chapter to write and we all need to get together and write it well.

Wendy's story personifies how Linda Lambert (1998) defines leadership: "Leadership is the reciprocal learning process that enables participants in a community to construct meaning toward a shared purpose" (p. 18).

The framework this book presents is designed to help create the kind of leadership that both Linda and Wendy talk about. Clearly, Hartland/Lakeside as a district and Wendy Lombard, as an individual contributor and leader within that district, have made a commitment to evolving their shared vision of what school should be (*focus*) by creating meaning out of their data (*reflection*) through dialogue and relationship building (*collaboration*).

Each of these components is evident in Wendy's message, but perhaps more importantly, her words suggest these elements will continue to evolve. The vision will become clearer as ongoing feedback and reflection illuminate the district's progress. Relationships will strengthen as people share their personal visions, values, and beliefs. Learning, on the part of both the adults and the children, will continue to drive an even deeper desire for new knowledge, self-improvement, and organizational excellence.

As we have emphasized, focus, reflection, and collaboration are not static, nor are they "events" that are scheduled and completed. They are dynamic, both individually and in their relationship to each other; each element creates energy and capacity for continuous growth within the organization. Lambert's definition of leadership capacity is all about the positive energy and learning-focused environment that result when focus, reflection, and collaboration continuously work together. As Figure 6.1 illustrates, we regard leadership capacity as the systemic outcome of the dynamic interaction of focus, reflection, and collaboration.

Margaret Wheatley, an expert on organizational change, addresses this same dynamic when she talks about the interrelationship of shared vision (*focus*), information (*reflection*), and relationships (*collaboration*), which she identifies as the core elements of organizational learning and perpetual growth. They are the lifeblood of a healthy, organic system that must continuously improve if it is to remain healthy (see Wheatley, 1992).

To illustrate this concept in yet another way, think about a jazz ensemble. If you've

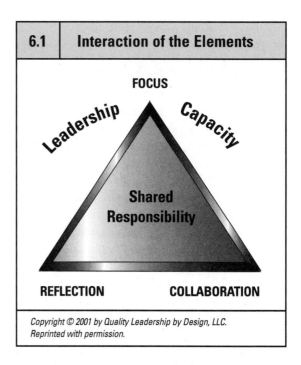

| 6.1 | Interaction of the Elements |

FOCUS

Leadership   Capacity

Shared Responsibility

REFLECTION   COLLABORATION

ever listened to jazz musicians create music through improvisation, you can appreciate the fundamental nature of organic systems. The musicians are guided by a combination of individual talent, self-discipline, and commitment, but also by the interactive and reciprocal relationship they have as members of the group. Although each brings unique beauty in the expression of his or her own music, it is the integration and interplay of all the parts flowing together that makes the end result so spectacular.

It's the same way with complex organizations like school systems (Dolan, 1994; Langford & Cleary, 1995; Senge, 2000; Wheatley, 1992). When working toward school improvement, everyone involved must understand how systems work and how each individual within the system contributes to the performance of the whole. It is also critical that everyone in the organization willingly take responsibility for the performance of the whole system. If any *one* of the jazz musicians chooses not to contribute or chooses to contribute in a way that is inherently dissonant, the end result would be compromised.

Wendy Lombard may never have read the works of the authors we've cited, but her remarks to her colleagues in the Hartland/Lakeside School District prove she understands how important it is to look for the big picture. To engage in leadership, Wendy knows she and her colleagues must become a part of the ongoing conversation about the vision, goals, progress, and effectiveness of their school district. And they must also be aware of how their individual actions contribute to the district's overall operation.

Wendy also knows that engaging in the work of leadership is something each person must choose to do. This is what we mean by shared responsibility. The element of choice is central to successful implementation of any reform initiative. McChesney and Hertling (2000) cite a study published in 1998 by Berends, Hielbrunn, McKelvey, and Sullivan that showed "when schools thoroughly research and freely choose designs, the level of implementation is higher than if the design is forced on the school staff, or if the staff has limited knowledge of the program" (p. 12).

Successful implementation of organizational change efforts also requires strong leadership on the part of positional leaders such as superintendents, central office administrators, and principals. Studies by Allen, Funkhouser, Kauffman, Kelliher, and Rusnak (1998) and Schaffer, Nesselrodt, and Stringfield (1997) show that school and district leaders play a vital role in promoting change and in supporting and directing activities that will help sustain the energy necessary to achieve the new vision throughout the system. It's this energy for continuous, ongoing improvement that Superintendent

Jeff Gruber was referring to as the hallmark of the Hartland/Lakeside district and the work of the committees he referenced.

However, as McChesney and Hertling (2000) point out, "Some researchers caution that reform efforts should not be dependent on the long term presence of a particular leader" (p.12). And educator, author, and historian Larry Cuban claims that the "innovations that have the best chance of sticking are those that have constituencies that grow around them" (O'Neil, 2000, p. 7). In other words, if an organization hopes to sustain change, it must commit to building capacity for broad-based participation in the ongoing transformational pursuit of the vision. The need for "leadership" to be independent of formal positional authority is what makes Lambert's definition of the concept so powerful, especially as it relates to building a culture of shared responsibility for student learning.

A key factor in Lambert's concept of leadership is the belief that learning and leadership are inextricably linked, continuously developed and deepened over time, and enhanced when they occur in community. Here are some additional assumptions we feel are inherent in the link between leading and learning:

• The opportunity to lead is inherently self-motivating.

• Everyone is capable of developing and exercising leadership.

• Leadership is expressed in a variety of ways.

• There are many domains within which leadership can be exercised.

• An organization's culture either supports or diminishes an individual's ability to demonstrate leadership.

• Enhancing individual leadership within a collaborative culture strengthens individual and organizational competence.

The rest of this chapter illustrates how the various roles within the system can contribute to the development and sustainability of leadership capacity. We will demonstrate how these assumptions play out within a culture of shared responsibility.

Roles, Responsibilities, and Skills for Building Leadership Capacity

Think back to the success story of Roosevelt Elementary School related in Chapter 1. Who is responsible for learning at Roosevelt? Answer: Everyone.

Working within a supportive system, teacher teams are taking the lead to learn from each other and continuously improve their instructional strategies. Instead of fearing the repercussions of their results, they learn from them. Teachers' time together is productive, purposeful, and focused on student learning. They have developed their skills in assessment, feedback, data gathering, data analysis, and dialogue. They support each other and are supported by a system that has made it possible for them to learn and improve together.

It's obvious Roosevelt teachers have been encouraged to act on their visions, solve problems among themselves, and take responsibility for effective use of resources. They take pride in the innovations they are implementing in their classrooms and in their own learning, as they adjust and improve upon their teaching strategies. They are professionals, accountable in every area, from budgeting to student performance to their own performance as a teaching team.

Furthermore, at Roosevelt, parents, staff, and students share in the responsibility for improving the learning environment. As leaders and problem-solvers, they are actively engaged in purposeful, important work that leads to the betterment of their school.

Lambert (1998) would refer to Roosevelt as a "Quadrant 4 school," one characterized by high skillfulness and high participation. This broad-based and skilled participation in the work of leadership translates into high leadership capacity. A lower-capacity school would be characterized by lesser levels of skill and limited participation. To illustrate the difference, let's consider the contrasting example of Eagle Ridge, a "Quadrant 1 school."

Eagle Ridge Elementary School

When the new principal of Eagle Ridge Elementary came on board, he brought with him ideals of high-capacity leadership and shared responsibility for student learning. One of the first things he said to his staff was, "I want this to be a place that doesn't need me in order to be successful."

Many months have passed. It's 2:45 on a Wednesday afternoon in April. Two teachers are standing in the hallway of Eagle Ridge Elementary, engaged in a heated discussion about the duplication of a lesson on dinosaurs that's taught at two different grade levels. The rights to the *Tyrannosaurus rex* unit have been a point of contention for six years, ever since the school expanded from a K–2 to a K–5 building. As the teachers carry on their debate, two classes of children are sitting unsupervised in the school gymnasium, waiting to be escorted to art and music following an all-school assembly.

No one had been assigned the responsibility of walking these students to their next class. The item was to be discussed during the faculty meeting held while students attended the assembly. But it never came up. The meeting was rushed, compressed into 45 minutes rather than the scheduled hour. (The start time was delayed 15 minutes because the principal was late returning from a district administrative team meeting. The rest of the staff couldn't begin without the principal because he was the only one who knew the meeting's agenda.) As a result, no decision was finalized about the transfer of students between special events and special classes. And so the children sit.

As the teachers continue their lively discussion about the dinosaur unit, four rambunctious girls dart back and forth between their classrooms and the bathroom. Finally, the school secretary comes out of the office, confronts the girls about the noise they are making, and sends them back to their classrooms.

When two of the girls return to class, their teacher reminds them of the hallway rules and tells them to return to their usual seats. The other girls' teacher sends them straight to the principal's office. There they wait while three parent volunteers receive instructions on which bulletin boards need to be taken down and redecorated for the coming season.

Down the hall, a small group of teachers is meeting to discuss the logistics of the school's Earth Day celebration. Elaine, who is relatively new at Eagle Ridge, brought the idea from her former school. The principal has enthusiastically given his blessing and has empowered the teachers to work out the details.

"Let's see, we'll need to contact the PTO to see if they can provide the brownies," Elaine says, consulting her checklist. "Who wants to do that?"

A reluctant volunteer raises his hand. Elaine continues, "There's going to be a chorus concert in the gym directly following the celebration. Do you think that will be a problem?"

"I don't know why it would be," offers one of several veteran faculty members. "The kids will already be there so we won't have to worry about moving them in and out." The teachers quickly agree there's no reason to be concerned. None of them know that the chorus teacher has made arrangements to have a mobile stage and lighting equipment hauled in an hour before the concert.

Who's responsible for learning at Eagle Ridge Elementary? Answer: No one in particular.

Eagle Ridge is a classic example of the unfocused, unproductive, and even negative energy often associated with change. There is little here to hang on to in the way of shared responsibility. Although the principal of Eagle Ridge sincerely wants the staff to share in the school's leadership, he has not done the work of building the staff's capacity for productive, skillful leadership. He has lost sight of the fact that there's a real need for *his* leadership, too. The principal has made two flawed assumptions: (1) that everyone at Eagle Ridge understands, is committed to, and has the skills necessary to exercise leadership; and (2) that everyone at Eagle Ridge is of one mind about where they are headed as a school community.

As our peek at daily life within Eagle Ridge reveals, reality has not matched this principal's expectations. Rather than the shared leadership he had anticipated, he finds that the staff is blaming him for what they perceived to be a complete *lack* of leadership. (After all, isn't that what he gets paid the big bucks to provide?) Meetings are chaotic and they do not start without him; decisions are not carried through or are simply not made; issues are left hanging; and conflicts continue to fester. People come and go. No one's sure who's in charge of what.

To make matters worse, when one or two people who have a passion for something choose to exercise leadership, their peers are critical and accuse them of receiving favorable treatment from the principal. Because their efforts at leadership are not connected to or coordinated with other staff, these attempts to introduce innovation end up as points of conflict rather than reasons for celebration.

There are all sorts of indicators of trouble. Parent contributions at Eagle Ridge are only minimally tapped; they are an extra pair of hands at best. Different teachers set different behavioral standards and consequences, meaning the children are getting mixed messages about what's okay and what is not. And although Eagle Ridge is in a district with plenty of resources and few barriers to academic success, its student achievement levels are ho-hum. What's more, nobody seems to notice.

The Gap Between Eagle Ridge and Roosevelt

There is a simple rule of thumb that says individuals within a work system have immediate and direct control over only about 15 percent of what they do. The remaining 85 percent of their work depends on the system being healthy and functioning as a coordinated, purposeful entity (see Deming, 1982).

This leads to us to a question: Where at Eagle Ridge is there the time, desire, or skill to focus on improved student learning? These elements are obviously present at Roosevelt Elementary School. The

contrasting examples these two schools provide illustrate what happens to the time and energy of teachers who work within systems that intentionally support capacity for leadership, learning, and change (Roosevelt) or unintentionally diminish it (Eagle Ridge).

What happened at Roosevelt that hasn't happened at Eagle Ridge? Were the teachers at Roosevelt born with more desire and a greater ability to lead? Are the teachers at Eagle Ridge less committed to learning? Or is there something within Roosevelt's culture that has liberated the natural desire for leadership in the hearts and minds of the staff?

Creating the Culture for Shared Responsibility and Leadership Capacity

What Roosevelt has that Eagle Ridge does not is a culture that supports and builds capacity for shared leadership and learning. Such a culture doesn't magically appear; it evolves through explicit and intentional work at defining, redesigning, and continuously improving every aspect of the way they do school.

Although every person within the organization has a role to play in initiating a culture of shared responsibility, Deal and Peterson (1999) focus special attention on principals. They assert that one of the most significant roles a principal can play is the "creation, encouragement, and refinement of the symbols and symbolic activity that give meaning to the organization . . . it is the important, informal aspects of their symbolic authority that often enable principals to exercise influence effectively" (p. 12). In short, "the only thing of real importance that leaders do is to create and manage culture" (Schein, 1997, p. 5).

Symbolism plays a powerful role in shaping culture. Walk into any school and immediately you will find symbols of what that school values. For example, you might see a trophy case in the front entryway, overflowing with medals, certificates, ribbons, and trophies documenting the school's history of athletic dominance. At a more enlightened school, the trophy case might shine the light on merit scholars and competitively successful debate teams and math clubs. And yet, both schools (unconsciously or not) are using symbolism to tell all who enter that this culture values winning.

On the other hand, think about a school that fills its halls and entryways with proudly displayed student work—and not just "the best work," but work from all levels, all subjects, all classes. This school is using symbols to communicate that learning is valued here. Pictures of staff, student, and parent teams symbolize the value placed on teamwork. Clean halls and quiet study areas symbolize safety and a respect for learning. Celebrations, art displays, and historical artifacts associated with multiple cultures symbolize the school's value of and respect for diversity. Visitor parking spaces near the school symbolize one set of values; reserved spaces labeled and lined up in order of positional power symbolize something quite different. There is no end to the symbolism that reflects school culture and it's important to understand the power those symbols have in shaping the future of our schools.

Because symbols stand for what is valued, they are highly resistant to change. Most symbols have been "earned" in some way or are such a deeply embedded piece of collective history that they become the artifacts of a school's self-image. Things like titles, contracts, and classrooms with windows all symbolize hard-earned victories or longevity and tenure. They are pieces of the past that help remind school personnel of their collective experience as an organization and of who they are and what they stand for.

The courageous leadership question to ask is, "Are the symbols of our culture consistent with our current values and with where we want to go in the future?" The courageous leadership role is to challenge the symbols that are not consistent with the espoused values of the organization.

Language can be as symbolic as trophy cases and parking spaces. In Figure 6.2, we have assembled actual quotes from principals, superintendents, and teachers at various "stages" of accepting their organization's transformation toward a culture of shared responsibility. See if you can determine from each speaker's language how "far along" he or she is on the road to accepting personal responsibility for student learning. Give each statement one of the following ratings: "H" for high degree of personal responsibility; "L" for low degree of personal responsibility; "F" for fearful; "E" for evolving; "D" for disinterested.

Although it's by no means a scientific way to measure a culture, people's words often reveal their assumptions about the organization and their commitment to improving it. Let's examine each of the statements in Figure 6.2.

Statement 1. *"Why do we have to be here? If my supervisor doesn't like what I'm doing, why doesn't she just tell me what to do? I can't do what I want to do anyway; they won't let me."* The speaker is a principal in a large urban district with a very top-down and bureaucratic structure. This individual is feeling completely powerless and somewhat fearful. If you gave this statement an "L" or an "F," you'd be correct. You may also have interpreted this statement as one

6.2	An Exercise in Decoding Symbolic Language

How would you characterize the culture of shared responsibility for learning at each speaker's school?

H = High degree of personal responsibility   **L** = Low degree of personal responsibility

F = Fearful   **E** = Evolving   **D** = Disinterested

_____ 1. "Why do we have to be here? If my supervisor doesn't like what I'm doing, why doesn't she just tell me what to do? I can't do what I want to do anyway; they won't let me."

_____ 2. "I'm beginning to see teachers doing this on their own time. That's an indicator that it's becoming internalized."

_____ 3. *Is your school improvement work making a difference?* "Yes." *How do you know?* "We asked the staff and parents and they're happy. They think we're meeting our goals."

_____ 4. "The discussion we had about our data raised questions about what's being taught in all the previous grades. Teachers now know they can't say that maybe the kids will get it next year. They know they're being depended on and they're making the changes on their own."

_____ 5. "We were told to improve math scores but that'll never happen." *Why not?* "Because of the kids we have and the rotten textbooks we have to use." *So you're telling me you've given up?* "No, it's just impossible." *Then I guess it is.*

_____ 6. "I've developed a rubric and SMART goal for my teachers to give me feedback on how I'm doing in supporting their work."

_____ 7. "My role won't change, but others are going to need training."

Copyright © 2001 by Quality Leadership by Design, LLC. Reprinted with permission.

---

of disinterest, which is probably also true. However, the deeper issue of feeling like a victim of the system with little or no control sometimes masks itself as disinterest.

Statement 2. *"I'm beginning to see teachers doing this on their own time. That's an indicator that it's becoming internalized."* These words come from a principal who has been working for two years to build leadership capacity in her school. She's finally beginning to see the fruits of her efforts. The correct response on this item is "E" for evolving.

Statement 3. *Is your school improvement work making a difference? "Yes." How do you know? "We asked the staff and parents and they're happy. They think we're meeting our goals."* This statement came from a conversation we had with two members of a school improvement planning council. By probing "How do you know?" we were trying to get at whether they actually had any data to support the claim that their efforts were making a difference. They seem content to accept that as long as people *think* that goals are being met and appear happy, that's good enough. We'd give this one a "D" for disinterested or perhaps an early "E" for evolving.

Statement 4. *"The discussion we had about our data raised questions about what's being taught in all the previous grades. Teachers now know they can't say that maybe the kids will get it next year. They know they're being depended on and they're making the changes on their own."* The individual speaking here is part of a staff that is fully engaged in sharing responsibility for student learning. Staff members not only know what's being taught, how students are doing, and that others are depending on them, they accept the responsibility and are empowered to act on what they are learning. This one gets an "H" for high levels of both individual and collective responsibility.

Statement 5. *"We were told to improve math scores but that'll never happen."* Why not? *"Because of the kids we have and the rotten textbooks we have to use."* So you're telling me you've given up? *"No, it's just impossible."* Then I guess it is. These words come from a principal within a system where no one is taking ownership for improving results. Obviously, resources are probably an issue, but more disconcerting is the attitude of complete helplessness. It appears that this principal sees *the students* as the problem. We'd give this an "L" or "F." A "D" would also be an appropriate answer.

Statement 6. *"I've developed a rubric and SMART goal for my teachers to give me feedback on how I'm doing in supporting their work."* Here we have a comment from a new principal (first year) who is hungry for feedback from his staff. This district has been working for two years to develop writing rubrics and SMART goals at all levels. He is modeling the use of those tools to support his own professional development, and by doing so, he is showing his staff that what they think and say matters to him. This statement deserves an "H."

Statement 7. *"My role won't change, but others are going to need training."* This quote comes from a superintendent in a district in the exploratory stages of examining their culture and using data to make decisions. Of course, not knowing much about this individual's current role and relationship with staff, it is possible that his role doesn't need to change. However, that's not likely. We're going with an "L" or a "D" on this one.

As these examples show, shared responsibility for student learning has many dimensions and evolves over time at different rates and in different ways. We'd like to walk you through the story of one district's journey from low to high levels of capacity for shared responsibility and leadership. To do so, we will return to Savanna Oaks Elementary School in Verona, Wisconsin—the school we described in the opening pages of this book; the school where the common answer to the question about who's responsible for learning is "I am."

Savanna Oaks didn't start out as a high-capacity school. It actually started out as a different school altogether—one called Stoner Prairie Elementary. Its staff was once divided by philosophy, allegiances, and all the naturally isolating symbols and structures that can exist in a school. Their history provides a rich explanation of how this school has evolved into the dynamic community of leaders and learners that it is today. However, what can't be recalled with precision are the countless hours of relationship-building, dialogue, conflict resolution, and planning that have brought this school to a different and better place. What follows is a synopsis of the major milestones of Savanna Oaks' journey toward shared responsibility, with notations about the roles various stakeholders played to support the transformational process.

A Journey Toward Shared Responsibility

In 1987, rapid growth in one part of the district led the Verona Area School District to build a new K–5 school called Stoner Prairie Elementary. The principal, Bill Conzemius, opened the new school and the new school year by asking the staff to reflect on this question: "If you could create the school of your dreams, what would it look like?" Bill asked them not to think just about the physical space, but what it would feel like, sound like, *be like* to "do school in a totally different way." This, he told his staff, would be the central focus of their conversations throughout the year.

"He talked about it all the time," one teacher recalls. "He relentlessly asked us to play it out in our minds and in our conversations." In faculty meetings, in grade-level teams, in one-on-one exchanges between staff members and the principal, the conversation centered on beliefs about learning, about each other, and about what they wanted as outcomes for their students.

Principal Role: *Convene the conversation and set the tone for visioning.*

When action didn't readily follow the dialogue, Bill found himself faced with a dilemma to which many principals can relate: Should he push for action or wait patiently for something to happen on its own? He had learned from his own research on change that unless there is a process teachers can use to initiate action and an environment that encourages innovation, change is not likely to occur (W. Conzemius, 1993). Knowing that one of the barriers to change is a lack of structured time to collaborate, plan, and learn together, Bill decided that something had

to change relative to how time was being used in his building.

Recall that since the mid-1980s, the Verona Area School District has given a substantial degree of decision-making authority to the school sites. Building on a philosophy that decisions about teaching and learning are best made by those closest to the action, the school board and central office administration developed (and in 1993, formally adopted) a governance policy that allocates 80 percent of budget decisions to school site councils.

Verona's school site councils are made up of parents, staff, principals, and in the upper grades, students. They are responsible for deciding staffing needs and patterns, school policies and procedures affecting student learning, and staff development strategies. School site councils are also responsible for developing the schools' operational plans. (See Appendix C for a more detailed discussion of systemwide planning within the Verona Area School District.)

Board and Central Office Role: *Build capacity for real, broad-based authority and decision making. Provide resources. Expect and support local action at the school site.*

School Site Council Role: *Develop schoolwide goals and plans. Challenge school policies and procedures that present barriers to learning. Design staff development to support goals. Allocate resources (as determined by district policy).*

To kick off the change process at his school, Bill asked the school site council for their help thinking through some strategies for creating time for teachers to plan collaboratively. The result? The council created a position for a full-time "planning sub," a certified teacher who could take over every classroom for one hour each week to give teachers time for individual reflection and planning. In addition, the council decided to hire five certified teachers to work as "permanent substitutes" three days each month, allowing each of the school's five-member teacher teams to hold a monthly half-day of group planning and sharing. Here the value is on collaboration for the purpose of alignment and continuity of curriculum and instruction, analyzing data, setting goals, monitoring progress, and creating new strategies for teaching and learning.

Principal Role: *Break down barriers. Deal with administrative and systems procedures so that teachers don't have to hassle with them.*

School Site Council Role: *Stay focused on system improvements to support better teaching and learning. Be creative.*

Two years passed before a group of teachers stepped up to the plate to take on the principal's challenge of creating the school of their dreams. Together, this group crafted a philosophy statement, which included a mission for a bold multi-age program (see Chapter 2), and developed curricular and instructional frameworks that included teachers working in teams with the same students for more than one year (see A. Conzemius, 1999). The program they envisioned would have a constructivist philosophy and would eliminate age-based grade levels and traditional letter grades; instead, teachers and parents would work collaboratively to design an assessment and reporting strategy based on developmental milestones and documented by demonstrations of student performance. In fall 1990, three years after Bill's initial challenge, the school launched the multi-age prototype as a pilot program in grades 1 through 3.

Teacher Role: *Take a chance! Act on your vision. Begin with a plan and be willing to test out your ideas before implementing them full*

scale (see Chapter 5's discussion of the PDSA learning cycle).

By the beginning of the 1993–94 school year, the Verona Area School District was taking bold steps toward a vision of shared responsibility. With increased levels of site autonomy provided by the district governance policy, Verona schools needed a mechanism that would allow them to function interdependently within the system. In an effort to maintain a system approach, the Verona Board of Education and central office administration turned the entire structure of accountability on its head. Within the context of the district's strategic plan, the sites were asked to develop goals, based on data gathered and analyzed at the classroom level. Those goals would become part of the site's overarching operational plan, to be presented to the board and central administration on an annual basis. Finally, the board and central office would use the collection of site-specific operational plans as the foundation for Verona's system goals.

Board and Central Office Role: *Create a mechanism for communicating, monitoring, and developing systemwide goals and measures.*

In 1996, in response to area population growth, the district constructed a new school, Savanna Oaks Elementary, on the same property as Stoner Prairie. Savanna Oaks would house students in grades 3–5 and Stoner Prairie's grade configuration would change from K–5 to K–2. This new organization presented a challenge for the now-thriving multi-age program, which had grown to serve a rapidly expanding number of children in grades 1–5. The site council and teachers decided the program would remain intact and would be housed in the new Savanna Oaks building.

The population of the Savanna Oaks/Stoner Prairie attendance area was both growing and diversifying. In just 5 years, the percentage of students receiving free or reduced-price lunch rose from 6 to 33 percent, and the percentage of minority students rose from 9 to 30 percent. Building on the legacy of teacher leadership first demonstrated by the founders of the multi-age program, and recognizing the need to address the increasingly different needs of an ever-changing population of students, the Savanna Oaks teachers took up the conversation about "dream schools" that had begun at Stoner Prairie.

Over time, however, staff divisions reemerged, and differing instructional philosophies and points of view threatened the school's sense of community. Bill Conzemius, now the principal at Savanna Oaks, asked another important question to get the community back on track: "Are we organized in a way that will best meet the needs of our changing population?"

Bill comments, "I wanted the teachers to really think about and decide for themselves what the best delivery system or systems should be." One of the first things the teachers did was to find out more about the changing needs of their student population by examining the data profiles of the children who were having the greatest difficulty. (See Chapter 3's discussion of the data–logic chain.)

Principal Role: *Refocus the conversation. Encourage teachers to challenge the status quo. Provide direction through inquiry and data.*

Teacher Role: *Examine the data. Challenge assumptions. Listen openly to parents, students, and each other to inform your decisions.*

Instead of allowing their differences to fuel conflict and division, the teachers at Savanna Oaks found ways to accept and accommodate their multiple perspectives and to align their visions of what a school should be. Today, the school maintains three distinct instructional options under one roof (see Chapter 2, page 25). Each program has a separate identity, a particular philosophy, and its own staff.

The school's multi-age program, transplanted from Stoner Prairie, is based on beliefs about constructivist learning, developmentally guided curriculum and instruction, and performance-based assessment. It operates literally around the corner and down the hall from the Core Knowledge Charter School, developed in 1996 by teachers and parents who value direct instruction and highly structured curriculum content and sequences. Finally, there is the "common" school, which uses more conventional grade structures and instructional methods. Even within this more traditional school model, teachers are working together quite differently than they did years ago and have grouped themselves into cross-graded teams to serve children and families over time.

According to Principal Bill Conzemius, Savanna Oaks' solution "is an idea whose time has come. We are dealing with a very diverse and mobile group of children. To assume you can capture all of them with one technique or strategy is incredibly naïve" (Carleton, 1996, p. A1).

The central role of student data is a distinguishing feature of the decision-making model at Savanna Oaks and in the Verona Area School District as a whole. Teachers regularly come together to examine and reflect on what their various sources of data are telling them about their students' progress. The district's bottom-up philosophy of goal setting emphasizes teachers' skills, knowledge, and professional capacity; it gives teachers the leading role in defining student needs and progress. Let's return to Savanna Oaks and see how the school transitioned to this role.

To begin the data-gathering and goal-setting process, Bill Conzemius and Monica Bischoff, the principal of Stoner Prairie, convened a collaborative meeting to look at how all students in the combined Stoner Prairie and Savanna Oaks attendance vicinity were performing in key areas of learning and behavior.

Faculty and staff from both schools examined a variety of data sources, including some standardized measures and some teacher-developed assessments. After a little initial resistance and a great deal of dialogue, the two schools agreed on a common goal: "Improve student achievement in reading and language arts." Next, grade-level and unit teams looked at their data to identify the specific gaps and skill sets they would need to focus on throughout the year to achieve the goal. Each group developed its own SMART goal, which then became the backbone of the schools' operational plans.

Principal Role: *Help grade-level and cross-grade–level teams understand and use data to develop results-based goals.*

Now let's follow our principals into a meeting where staff teams from Savanna Oaks and Stoner Prairie are working on their goals. This is the second of five "30+ Minute Meetings" devoted to goal setting (see page 105). The teachers are gathered around tables, charts in hand, heads together. Their task focus is intense. One teacher jumps up to get a flipchart to capture her team's freely flowing ideas. After about 20 minutes, someone calls time, and the teams move into the next phase—determining which goal area they want to work on and how they will measure their

progress. By the end of the meeting, each team has agreed on a goal and has made a plan for conducting the research that will determine the best practices they will employ to achieve this goal.

Teacher Role: *Participate and engage in the goal-setting and data analysis process. Embrace the role of a lifelong learner.*

It's now mid-October, and the boardroom at the Verona district headquarters is beginning to fill with teachers and parents. Tonight's meeting will present the school operational plans for Stoner Prairie and Savanna Oaks. Principals Bischoff and Conzemius step forward to share the schools' goals for the coming year.

First, the data: Several years of standardized test scores show that these two schools have kept pace with the other elementary schools in the district, even though they serve a much more diverse student population. The principals explain that because their data forecast that student populations at Stoner Prairie and Savanna Oaks will continue to diversify, the schools have decided to place their greatest focus this year on reading and language arts. Both have set schoolwide goals of improving student performance in these two areas.

Then, one by one, the grade-level teams step forward to present their goals. The Early Childhood (pre-K) team announces its decision to work on oral vocabulary development. Kindergarten teachers have set a goal of improving upper- and lower-case letter recognition to 80-percent mastery. The 1st grade team's goal takes this farther: "Improve students' phonemic awareness to an average of 90 percent on the dictated-sentence assessment." Stoner Prairie Principal Monica Bischoff explains that the Early Childhood, kindergarten, and 1st grade teachers will be working with Title I and the reading specialist to develop new instructional and program materials based on these goals.

The board members nod in approval. By the end of the night, they will have heard SMART goals for all grade levels at the paired schools, as well as the SMART goals set for the multi-age and core knowledge programs, pupil services, and the related arts. All the teams have identified areas of need based on student performance data they've gathered and analyzed.

Following the complete round of school site presentations, the board reviews all school operational plans as a way to inform its systemwide goal-setting process. In this way, the Verona Area School District sets and monitors long-range strategic goals based on the classroom data that have bubbled up from each school's goal-setting process. Thanks to a board-defined policy on assessment, planning, and governance structures for all the sites, Verona's board is confident that it has a clear picture of the whole system and can make informed decisions and plans based on the data.

Board Role: *Listen. Encourage. Inquire. Develop strong policy language and a clearly articulated philosophy on how data will be used in the system.*

What lesson can educators learn from this success story? As mentioned earlier, every school's story will be different, *must* be different, because every school has a unique culture and community, unique individuals, and a unique vision. But what all educators can conclude from this example—and can transport to other settings—is the understanding that good processes for creating focus and engaging broad-based leadership in reflective practices and collaborative problem solving lead to shared responsibility for

student learning. When the framework for shared responsibility is alive and well, not only will all members of the school community say, "I'm responsible," they'll add, "And I'd never go back to the way it was before. This is a better place to be."

Reflections: Systemic Support for Change

Savanna Oaks' positive journey represents only a small part of the Verona Area School District's complete transformation from a school system to a *system of schools*. Verona's vision emerged over several years, from hours of conversation among the system's many stakeholders. It was built on a set of beliefs about learning, core values, and a commitment to the district's mission. However, as the district's vision began to evolve into greater clarity, it became obvious that change was necessary at every level of the system. Everyone seemed to understand that if they did not challenge the current system, they could expect only modest changes that would not be worth their time. (Appendix D provides a self-assessment that can help you begin looking at your own district.)

The educational literature abounds with research and best practices for systemic and cultural change (see Deal & Peterson, 1999; Dolan, 1994; Fullan, 1991, 1993, 1999; Sarason, 1990). We couldn't possibly capture in one small portion of this book the wisdom and the volume of work these authors have contributed to educators' understanding of school improvement. However, the Verona story certainly illustrates the basic tenets of the systemic change process and deserves its mention here.

W. Patrick Dolan (1994) was a highly influential force in the early stages of Verona's transformation. With his guidance, Verona convened a districtwide "Educational Forum" that served as the "scaffold" of support for the change process. The Forum continues to this day and is now focused on continuous improvement. It includes members of the district board, the unions, and central and site administration as well as representatives from school site teams—teachers, support staff, parents, and students.

In the beginning, this group's role was to provide a place for the system to listen, learn, and give permission for change to begin. Sometimes this meant providing waivers from contract or policy language. At other times, the Forum simply provided an arena for discussion and relationship building. Through this process, it became clear that before Verona's vision could become a reality, the system and its stakeholders needed to create support mechanisms, redefine roles, and develop skills. We'd like to share briefly some of the important things they've learned.

The Role of Administrators

Central administration has a critical role to play in creating the systemic support mechanisms that encourage and facilitate the change process. For example, each school site needs to learn about what other sites in the system are doing to improve learning. Central office administration must lead by creating the place, time, and expectation for interschool connections that will support systemwide learning. In addition, superintendents and central office directors need to redefine their roles in ways that will allow site-based leadership teams to flourish. Some of the central administration's more important change-supporting functions include

- Eliminating system barriers to innovation.
- Facilitating the development of systemwide standards.

- Developing a district assessment plan.
- Providing strategic staff development.
- Coordinating data analysis for the sites to use in their planning.

New skills are another imperative for administrators. Generally, principals, central office directors, and superintendents who value broad-based participation must be able to engage the rest of their teams in the work of leadership and learning. The knowledge base and skill set required for facilitating the process of change has become an absolute must in today's work environments. Schein (1997) describes "learning" cultures as those best able to make their own continual diagnosis and self-manage whatever transformations are necessary to keep pace with environmental changes. "The challenge lies in conceptualizing a culture of innovation in which learning, adaptation, innovation, and perpetual change are the stable elements" (Schein, 1997, p. xiv).

Positional leaders must not only believe in and engage people in change, they must understand the *need* for change and facilitate a *process* for change. Bill Conzemius (1993) investigated the knowledge and skills characteristic of principals leading change and the stages of acceptance school staff experience when they are asked to participate in change. In a study involving 304 teachers and administrators from 14 school districts, he found dramatically different patterns of change acceptance between administrators and staff—patterns that remained constant regardless of the kind of change being proposed. The study showed that of the two groups, administrators were generally much more comfortable with the idea of change. More importantly, 100 percent of the administrators surveyed profoundly misjudged staff beliefs about the most essential elements of change management.

According to the principals and superintendents, what staff needed most to manage change was more information about the particular innovations being introduced. In reality, teachers were far more concerned about *how* the change would be implemented and the impact the change would have on themselves and on their work. Many teachers were convinced their ideas for system improvement were better than the changes proposed by administration, but noted that they had not been asked to share these ideas.

Interestingly, 75 percent of the administrators surveyed agreed or strongly agreed that staff had adequate opportunity for input, yet over 55 percent of the staff felt that they did not have adequate opportunity to participate. This finding suggests positional leaders need to be more open to feedback about how they are including all staff, parents, and students in the important decisions affecting teaching and learning, and they need to adjust their actions accordingly.

The Role of Teachers

Teachers can support the change process (and one another) by participating in peer study teams, offering each other relevant and constructive feedback, and showing interest in each other's successes. They need to learn the leadership skills of dialogue, meeting facilitation, group decision making, and group problem solving. They also must know how to gather data on an ongoing basis so they can adjust their teaching strategies accordingly.

It is our firm belief that given time, support, and encouragement from the system, teachers will choose to share in the responsibility for improving student learning.

That is what real leadership is all about. And that is what brought teachers to their profession in the first place.

Summary: Leadership

Shared responsibility for student learning requires leadership capacity—the skill and the will to engage all stakeholders in the system's sustained, continuous improvement. For organizations as complex as schools to remain vital, dynamic, and healthy, everyone working within the system must align their vision of learning. This is only possible when the entire system engages in the processes of *focus, reflection,* and *collaboration.*

Until we educators take a serious look at the elements of existing school culture that either support or diminish shared responsibility for student learning, leadership will remain the purview of a chosen few. Building shared responsibility and leadership capacity will require role changes, skill development, and participation at every level of the educational organization. We will see real and lasting reform—and significant, sustained improvement of student results— only when individuals, guided by a clear moral purpose, come together to challenge the assumptions of the system as we have come to know it.

Building shared responsibility for student learning is an ongoing, iterative journey, filled with unanticipated turns and unexpected side roads. Regardless of the manner in which your journey unfolds, you will gain great wisdom from the experience. Most importantly, your students will benefit. Enjoy your travels.

Tree Diagram for SMART Reading Goals (Elementary)

Results Goal	Indicators	Measures	Targets	SMART Goals
Improve reading comprehension of all 2nd and 3rd grade students.	Students comprehend words or phrases essential to the meaning of the story.	Terra Nova Test	Increase mastery from 8% to 50% (currently, 8% of students are at mastery).	By the end of the school year, 50% of students will show mastery of word comprehension on the Terra Nova 2nd grade reading test.
		In-class vocabulary-assessment	Increase from 15 to 45 students (currently only 15 students consistently score 100%).	By the end of this semester, at least 45 students (out of 60 total) will consistently achieve 100% on the in-class vocabulary assessment.
	Students recognize major points made in the text as well as structural relationships such as compare/contrast, cause/effect, and outlining.	Terra Nova Test	Increase mastery from 15% to 50% (currently 15% of students are at mastery).	By the end of the school year, 50% of students will show mastery in their ability to recognize major points made in text and structural relationships in text.
		In-class comprehension assessment (leveled texts)	Decrease errors by 50%.	Within 6 weeks, each student will have reduced the number of comprehension errors they are making by 50%.

Tree Diagram for SMART Writing Goals (Middle)

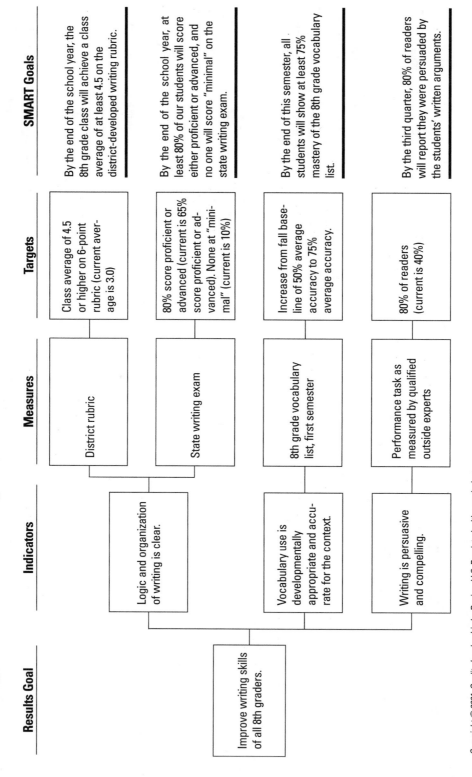

Results Goal	Indicators	Measures	Targets	SMART Goals
Improve writing skills of all 8th graders.	Logic and organization of writing is clear.	District rubric	Class average of 4.5 or higher on 6-point rubric (current average is 3.0)	By the end of the school year, the 8th grade class will achieve a class average of at least 4.5 on the district-developed writing rubric.
		State writing exam	80% score proficient or advanced (current is 65% score proficient or advanced). None at "minimal" (current is 10%)	By the end of the school year, at least 80% of our students will score either proficient or advanced, and no one will score "minimal" on the state writing exam.
	Vocabulary use is developmentally appropriate and accurate for the context.	8th grade vocabulary list, first semester	Increase from fall baseline of 50% average accuracy to 75% average accuracy.	By the end of this semester, all students will show at least 75% mastery of the 8th grade vocabulary list.
	Writing is persuasive and compelling.	Performance task as measured by qualified outside experts	80% of readers (current is 40%)	By the third quarter, 80% of readers will report they were persuaded by the students' written arguments.

Copyright © 2001. Quality Leadership by Design, LLC. Reprinted with permission.

Tree Diagram for SMART Analytical Thinking Goals (High)

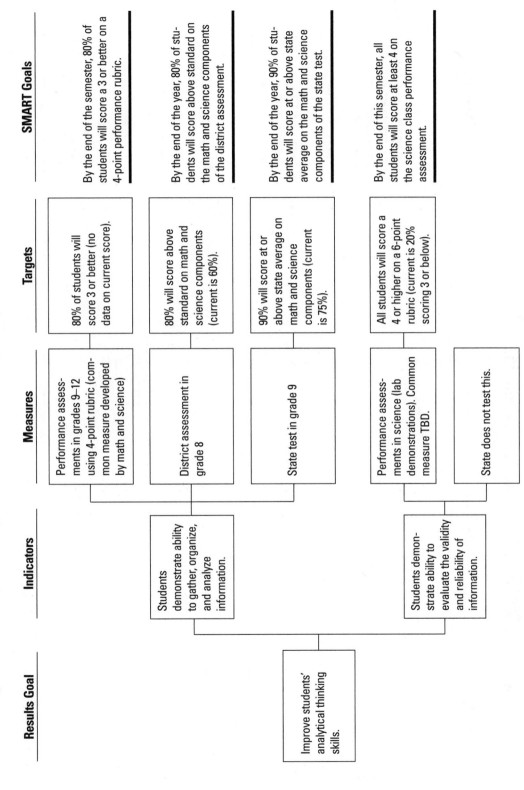

Results Goal	Indicators	Measures	Targets	SMART Goals
Improve students' analytical thinking skills.	Students demonstrate ability to gather, organize, and analyze information.	Performance assessments in grades 9–12 using 4-point rubric (common measure developed by math and science)	80% of students will score 3 or better (no data on current score).	By the end of the semester, 80% of students will score a 3 or better on a 4-point performance rubric.
		District assessment in grade 8	80% will score above standard on math and science components (current is 60%).	By the end of the year, 80% of students will score above standard on the math and science components of the district assessment.
		State test in grade 9	90% will score at or above state average on math and science components (current is 75%).	By the end of the year, 90% of students will score at or above state average on the math and science components of the state test.
	Students demonstrate ability to evaluate the validity and reliability of information.	Performance assessments in science (lab demonstrations). Common measure TBD.	All students will score a 4 or higher on a 6-point rubric (current is 20% scoring 3 or below).	By the end of this semester, all students will score at least 4 on the science class performance assessment.
		State does not test this.		

Tree Diagram for SMART Climate Goals (Schoolwide)

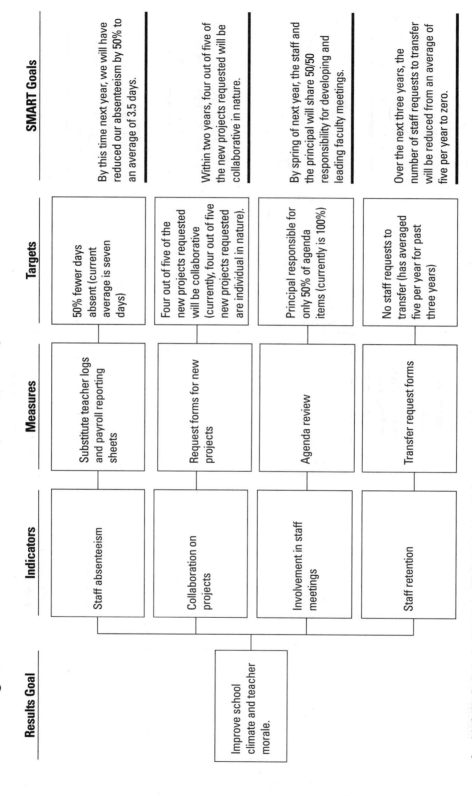

Results Goal	Indicators	Measures	Targets	SMART Goals
Improve school climate and teacher morale.	Staff absenteeism	Substitute teacher logs and payroll reporting sheets	50% fewer days absent (current average is seven days)	By this time next year, we will have reduced our absenteeism by 50% to an average of 3.5 days.
	Collaboration on projects	Request forms for new projects	Four out of five of the new projects requested will be collaborative (currently, four out of five new projects requested are individual in nature).	Within two years, four out of five of the new projects requested will be collaborative in nature.
	Involvement in staff meetings	Agenda review	Principal responsible for only 50% of agenda items (currently is 100%)	By spring of next year, the staff and the principal will share 50/50 responsibility for developing and leading faculty meetings.
	Staff retention	Transfer request forms	No staff requests to transfer (has averaged five per year for past three years)	Over the next three years, the number of staff requests to transfer will be reduced from an average of five per year to zero.

 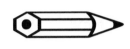

Name **Susan Olson**

School Mazomanie   Year 2000

Assignment/Grade Unit A

Individual Goal

1. Rewrite and update the current 1st grade report card to better reflect what is being taught and assessed in the classroom.

Rationale

1. Report cards need to be updated so that they are more in line with the standards and reflect the benchmarks that we need to achieve.

Related Goals/Activities

Building Goal: Improve communication   Wisconsin Teacher Standards: Standard #8 assessment

District Goal: Invest in Partnerships

Committee Membership/Activity

Science Committee; Environmental Education Committee.

Indicator

1. Report card revision done in time for the first grading period
2. Survey parents on how they like the new report card

3. Quarterly reassessment of report card by teacher

4. Alignment of the report card with the State Standards and benchmarks for grade 1.

Measurement

1. Completed revisions to secretary for typing by October 9, 2000.
2. Develop a survey to hand out at conferences (turn in by November 3, 2000).
3. List possible revisions to report card two weeks after each grading period.

4. Compare and list concepts taught and information reported on the report cards with the Standards benchmarks by the end of the school year. Which benchmarks are not included? List.

Achievement

1. Given to the secretary on 10/4/00.
2. Survey letter completed on 10/6/00.

3. To be submitted to the site council team by the end of the second quarter.
4. Alignment completed on 10/11/00.

Courtesy of the Wisconsin Heights School District.

Components of the Verona Area School District Strategic Plan

Planning in the Verona Area School District (VASD) captures two components:

- The listening and governance structures reach to engage all corners of the community in the conversation about the schools.
- A nonlinear approach to planning has established a framework that forms the boundary of discussion, innovation, and implementation across the district.

These components ensure the system is stable, reflects the needs and hopes of the community, and gives everyone an opportunity to use personal talents and gifts to build excellence. The resulting framework has five areas:

1. An **Educational Plan** delineating mission, beliefs, learning and character goals, learning environments, and standards and assessments.
2. **Inclusive governance structures** ensuring decisions close to the point of action through participatory processes while maintaining systemic accountability.
3. **Site-based fiscal management** that empowers each site by placing planning and management for over 80 percent of district resources in the hands of shared decision-making councils in each school.
4. A **technology platform focused on learning**, which provides tools necessary to customize instruction while creating a powerful student-based data system that guides planning.
5. **Long-range planning** for growth, fiscal needs, and education programming that keeps the district renewed toward the future.

1. The Educational Plan

The Educational Plan, shaped by the VASD's mission and goals, is the driving force of the framework.

Mission: The Verona Area School District, a community of learners, values and supports educational excellence. To foster the joy of learning and to prepare students for future challenges, we set rigorous academic and creative expectations for each student. Students, in turn, must show they meet these expectations.

Reprinted by permission of the Verona Area School District, Verona, Wisconsin.

As a result of this mission, the VASD has developed both learning and character goals:

• **Goal:** Curriculum content is aligned with district standards and assessments. By passing a student to another grade or granting a minimum passing grade, the teacher validates that the student demonstrated at least a minimal acceptable competency of aligned standards.

• **Goal:** By June 2003, each student will demonstrate proficiency in meeting the VASD's academic standards at every grade level and make significant gains in learning each year (as measured by norm- and criterion-referenced measures or performance assessments).

• **Goal:** Each graduate will meet rubrics delineating character goals in the areas of person, family or friend, steward, citizen, and producer. Work on these goals is collected, often in portfolios, and communicated regularly and used in personal assessment and planning with students.

The VASD has achieved a constancy of vision by submitting its mission and goals to broad community review. As a result, the mission and goals have remained constant for nearly 10 years. During that time, instructional planning throughout the district and within each site has moved from outcome-based to standards-based formats.

2. Inclusive Governance Structures

Governance structures enable all corners of the district to engage in conversations about teaching and learning, harnessing the unique talents and gifts of all individuals, and creating customized learning opportunities for children based on varied philoso-

phies developed to the highest standard. There are four key structures:

i. **Board of Education:** The Board is legally defined as the elected decision-making body in the VASD. Without abdicating its authority, the Board has increasingly moved decision-making closer to the point of action. Simultaneously, the Board has increased its focus on broad policy, fiscal, and philosophy issues that influence district climate and culture.

ii. **Districtwide Educational Forum:** The districtwide educational forum was created by the Board. The Forum consists of 38 members representing staff and parents from each site, students, community members at large, union representatives, and administration. It exists to ensure that decision-making bodies throughout the district have the opportunity to listen to all points of view from all corners of the community. The Forum meets monthly to discuss the topics of greatest concern to the district; these discussions help inform site leaders and the Board.

iii. **Site Councils:** Site councils were created by the Board to engage local representatives in decision making through collaborative learning, planning, listening, and sharing. Each Site Council meets regularly to . . .

• Focus on student learning at the site.

• Serve as a forum for diverse perspectives from the school, home, and community to ensure the exchange of a variety of viewpoints.

• Provide participatory shared decision-making at each site to create the individual school's structure and culture (within the district Framework).

- Promote communication between parents, community members, professional and support personnel, students, and administration.

iv. **Accountability:** Accountability of each site to the district is assured through policies that require annual reports to the Board. Charter schools must submit Annual Reports to the Board by August 1 of each year; noncharter sites must submit a Plan of Operation by the same date. All reports should have the following components:

- Assessment of the operations of the Site Council during the year.
- Report on student learning progress relative to common district standards and assessments (in addition to any unique site-specific measures).
- Status of work on current site goals and initiatives.
- Review of future site goals and initiatives.

3. Site-Based Fiscal Management

Beginning with the 1993–94 budget, planning and decision-making for instructional operations is shifted to the Site Councils. Instructional costs are distributed to the sites on a per-pupil basis. Decisions about site budget allocations must fall within the district framework; plans should be reported according to a template for fiscal planning developed in 1997. The three highest priorities for fiscal planning are:

i) Reduce class size in the first four years of school.

ii) Bring added resources to students at their point of readiness for learning.

iii) Build staff expertise.

4. Technology

Effective utilization of new technologies is necessary to support the broad-based, collaborative vision of the VASD. To bring accountability deep into the system at the individual, classroom, site, and district levels, an extensive multi-platform interactive database has been created and a fiber network installed to each classroom to provide Internet and E-mail access to all. An Oracle database allows staff to access relational data across formats and platforms. In recognition that the needs of the individuals using the machines has a greater impact on use and effectiveness than the machines themselves, each site has a technology assistant whose job is to keep the system simple and working for each classroom. Each site also has a professional educational technology coordinator whose sole job is to help staff and students bring the powers of the new technologies into the service of daily learning.

5. Long-Range Planning

The VASD is a dynamic, quickly growing, and changing district; it is crucial that the district effectively plan for future eventualities. As a result, the VASD has implemented a planning process that has moved away from year-to-year goal setting and planning. The new process establishes three- to five-year targets, which are reassessed each year and moved forward to the next year. The practice of planning in the long view with flexible future target dates enables the district to move the horizon to a higher level.

Self-Assessment: Attributes of a Culture of Shared Responsibility

Purpose: The purpose of this self-assessment is to determine the extent to which your school district's current culture supports shared responsibility for learning.

Instructions: For each of the categories that follow, circle the number that best reflects your perception of your district's culture. If you do not know, place an "X" in the box under the "Don't know" heading corresponding to that item.

Scoring Directions: Add up the total score for each category and transfer it to the table below. Items answered "Don't know" have no point value, but should be noted for further discussion. After completing per-category scoring, add these totals together to find the Assessment Sum Total.

Category	Total Score in Category	Number of items answered "Don't know"
Structures		
Systems		
Style		
Skills		
Symbols		
Assessment Sum Total:		

What the Scores Mean: The highest total score possible in each category is 40. Categories receiving scores of 16 or less are the areas of greatest need. Those receiving scores between 17 and 32 should be considered areas of relative strength. Categories receiving scores from 33 to 40 reflect exemplary learning cultures.

The highest total score possible is 200. Sum Total scores in the range of 0 to 80 indicate a need to redefine major aspects of district culture. Scores of 81 to 160 indicate a good foundation for shared responsibility, with some potential areas for change. Scores of 161 to 200 reflect exemplary learning cultures.

If you have marked "Don't know" for more than four items per category, we recommend that your district employ organizational development and communications strategies to increase awareness and invite dialogue among the stakeholders. People within a system cannot learn together and share responsibility for student learning if they are unaware of the cultural mores and patterns that influence their behaviors.

Self-Assessment: Structures

Examining the way we organize ourselves to do work.

Circle the number that best reflects your perception of your district's culture. If you do not know, place an "X" in the box under the "Don't know" heading corresponding to that item.

Descriptor	Not at all	A little bit	Some	Quite a lot	Very much	Don't know
1. The way in which we are organized supports team/organizational learning.	1	2	3	4	5	❑
2. There is a common understanding of where we are headed as a district.	1	2	3	4	5	❑
3. The organizational structure enhances our ability to think and problem solve systemically.	1	2	3	4	5	❑
4. The structure of the school day and year provides sufficient flexibility and time for staff, faculty, and administration to work together on instructional, curricular, programmatic, and process improvements.	1	2	3	4	5	❑
5. Staff, faculty, and administration have ample opportunity to learn from each other, to reflect and dialogue about professional matters, and to work collaboratively to improve their practice.	1	2	3	4	5	❑
6. Individuals within the district tend to view it as a whole as opposed to a collection of separate factions (i.e., jobs, grade levels, content areas).	1	2	3	4	5	❑
7. New knowledge and information are transferred quickly, efficiently, and accurately throughout the organization.	1	2	3	4	5	❑
8. All system stakeholders are adequately involved in goal setting and planning.	1	2	3	4	5	❑
Totals:						

Self-Assessment: Systems

Examining the set of processes we use to deliver services and carry out mission.

Circle the number that best reflects your perception of your district's culture. If you do not know, place an "X" in the box under the "Don't know" heading corresponding to that item.

Descriptor	Not at all	A little bit	Some	Quite a lot	Very much	Don't know
1. There is a well-defined process and parameters for shared decision making at all levels.	1	2	3	4	5	❑
2. Communications inside and outside the district are efficient and effective.	1	2	3	4	5	❑
3. Policies, procedures, and resource allocations are aligned with goals.	1	2	3	4	5	❑
4. There is a system in place for continuously improving all aspects of the teaching and learning environment.	1	2	3	4	5	❑
5. Staff meetings are participatory; teachers and support staff are actively involved in the design, delivery, and discussions at regularly scheduled meetings.	1	2	3	4	5	❑
6. Resource allocations are determined collaboratively at the site, where appropriate.	1	2	3	4	5	❑
7. Processes, operations, policies, and procedures that become obsolete or hinder the continued growth of the system and the people within it are systematically removed, improved, or replaced.	1	2	3	4	5	❑
8. Processes, operations, policies, and procedures are designed to be adaptive, flexible, and responsive.	1	2	3	4	5	❑
Totals:						

Self-Assessment: Style

Examining the manner with which we trust one another in our daily interactions.

Circle the number that best reflects your perception of your district's culture. If you do not know, place an "X" in the box under the "Don't know" heading corresponding to that item.

Descriptor	Not at all	A little bit	Some	Quite a lot	Very much	Don't know
1. People encourage one another to try new things and to share what they have learned.	1	2	3	4	5	❏
2. My opinions are valued and taken into consideration when decisions are being made.	1	2	3	4	5	❏
3. The faculty, staff, and administration work together in an informal, collegial, and open manner.	1	2	3	4	5	❏
4. A general feeling of trust permeates the organization, making risk taking, change, and improvement positive aspects of our district's culture.	1	2	3	4	5	❏
5. I am trusted to make judgments about my daily work activities.	1	2	3	4	5	❏
6. The environment encourages dialogue about the results we are achieving both individually and collectively.	1	2	3	4	5	❏
7. People feel free to speak their minds about what they have learned without fear of repercussions.	1	2	3	4	5	❏
8. There is a willingness to break old patterns of thinking and doing in order to find better ways of serving students and families.	1	2	3	4	5	❏
Totals:						

Self-Assessment: Skills

Examining the collective capacity of the organization to obtain the results it desires.

Circle the number that best reflects your perception of your district's culture. If you do not know, place an "X" in the box under the "Don't know" heading corresponding to that item.

Descriptor	**Not at all**	**A little bit**	**Some**	**Quite a lot**	**Very much**	**Don't know**
1. We constantly seek better ways to improve student learning.	1	2	3	4	5	❑
2. We know how effectively our current practices work and continuously seek to understand how new methods impact student performance.	1	2	3	4	5	❑
3. The district might be described as skilled in a collective sense; i.e., not only are the individuals competent, but the organization as a whole is successful in meeting its mission.	1	2	3	4	5	❑
4. Staff development is linked to the strategic objectives of the district.	1	2	3	4	5	❑
5. There is a system in place for everyone to learn from our experiences, past history, and best practices of others.	1	2	3	4	5	❑
6. Cross-district learning opportunities are expected and organized on a regular basis.	1	2	3	4	5	❑
7. People look forward to improving their own competencies and the competencies of the whole organization.	1	2	3	4	5	❑
8. The unexpected is viewed as an opportunity for learning.	1	2	3	4	5	❑
Totals:						

Self-Assessment: Symbols

Examining the images, ceremonies, rituals, and language that stand for what is valued.

Circle the number that best reflects your perception of your district's culture. If you do not know, place an "X" in the box under the "Don't know" heading corresponding to that item.

Descriptor	Not at all	A little bit	Some	Quite a lot	Very much	Don't know
1. What is said is what is done. Our leaders' behaviors reflect stated values.	1	2	3	4	5	❑
2. Communication tools and methods reflect or symbolize an underlying value of shared vision and team learning.	1	2	3	4	5	❑
3. Ceremonies, rituals, and celebrations are an important part of defining the uniqueness of the culture.	1	2	3	4	5	❑
4. It is okay to challenge "what is" if it's likely to produce better results for students.	1	2	3	4	5	❑
5. Organizational symbols reflect learning as a core value of the culture.	1	2	3	4	5	❑
6. Recognition and reward systems support a team approach.	1	2	3	4	5	❑
7. What is espoused in written and verbal communications is what is lived by those within the culture.	1	2	3	4	5	❑
8. Multiple viewpoints and open productive debates about organizational symbols are encouraged and cultivated.	1	2	3	4	5	❑
Totals:						

Bibliography

Allen, S., Funkhouser, J., Kauffman, D., Kelliher, K., & Rusnak, K. (1998). *Implementing schoolwide programs: Vol. 2. Profiles of successful schoolwide programs.* Washington, DC: United States Department of Education. (ERIC Document Reproduction Service No. ED 429 360)

Ambrose, D. (1987). *Managing complex change.* Philadelphia: The Enterprise Group, LTD.

Barth, P., Haycock, K., & Jackson, H. (Eds.). (1999). *Dispelling the myth: High poverty schools exceeding expectations.* (Report No. SR9901). Washington, DC: Education Trust. (ERIC Document Reproduction Service No. ED 445 140)

Berends, M., Heilbrunn, J., McKelvey, C., & Sullivan, T. (1998). *Monitoring the progress of new American schools: A description of implementing schools in a longitudinal sample.* Santa Monica, CA: RAND.

Bohm, D. (1992). On dialogue. *Noetic Sciences Review, 23,* 16–18.

Bonhoeffer, D. (1954). *Life together.* NY: Harper & Row Publishers, Inc.

Carleton, G. (1996, November 30). Three schools in one. *The Capital Times* (Madison, WI), A1, A3.

Cawelti, G. (1999). *Portraits of six benchmark schools: Diverse approaches to improving student achievement.* Arlington, VA: Educational Research Service.

Conzemius, A. (1999, Fall). Ally in the Office. *Journal of Staff Development, 20*(4), 31–34.

Conzemius, A. (2000). Framework. *Journal of Staff Development, 21*(1), 38–41.

Conzemius, W. C. (1993). *An exploratory study of the principles of Deming's theory of management in public schools involved in reform.* Unpublished doctoral dissertation, University of Wisconsin, Madison.

Deal, T. E. & Peterson, K. D. (1999). *Shaping school culture.* San Francisco: Jossey-Bass.

Deming, W. E. (1982). *Out of the crisis.* Cambridge: Massachusetts Institute of Technology.

Doherty, K. & Abernathy, S. (1998). *Turning around low performing schools: A guide for state and local leaders.* Washington, DC: United States Department of Education. (ERIC Document Reproduction Service No. ED 419 301)

Dolan, W. P. (1994). *Restructuring our schools: A primer on systemic change.* Kansas City, MO: Systems and Organization.

DuFour, R. (1995, April). Restructuring is not enough. *Educational Leadership, 52*(7), 33–36.

DuFour, R. & Eaker, R. E. (1998). *Professional learning communities at work.* Bloomington, IN: National Education Service.

Educational Research Service. (1999). School improvement: Factors leading to success or failure. *ERS Informed Educator Series.* Arlington, VA: Author.

Fullan, M. G. (1991). *The new meaning of educational change.* New York: Teachers College Press.

Fullan, M. G. (1993). *Change forces: Probing the depths of educational reform.* Philadelphia: Palmer Press.

Fullan, M. G. (1999). *Change forces: The sequel.* Philadelphia: Palmer Press.

Garmston, R. & Wellman, B. (1999). *The adaptive school: Developing and facilitating collaborative groups.* Norwood, MA: Christopher-Gordon Publishing.

Gonzalez, P., Calsyn, C., Jocelyn, L., et al. (2000). *Pursuing excellence: Comparisons of international eighth-grade mathematical and science achievement from a U.S. perspective, 1995 and 1999.* Washington, DC: National Center for Education Statistics.

Hall, A. & Erickson, E. (2000, October 24). Black and hispanic students narrow the gap. *Wisconsin State Journal* (Madison, WI), A1.

Herman, R. & Stringfield, S. (1997). *Ten promising programs for educating all children: Evidence of impact.* Arlington, VA: Educational Research Service.

Hoff, D. J. (2000, January 26). Testing's ups and downs predictable. *Education Week, 19*(20), 1, 12–13.

Jewell, L. N. & Reitz, H. J. (1981). *Group effectiveness in organizations.* Glenview, IL: Scott Foresman.

Johnson, J. F. (1998, June 29). *The promise of school reform in Texas.* Paper presented at a meeting of the Poverty and Race Research Action Council, Washington, DC.

Juran, J. (1995). *Managerial breakthrough* (Rev. ed.). New York: McGraw-Hill.

King, M. B. & Newmann, F. M. (2000, April). Will teacher learning advance school goals? *Phi Delta Kappan, 81*(8), 576–580.

Lambert, L. (1998). *Building leadership capacity in schools.* Alexandria, VA: Association for Supervision and Curriculum Development.

Lambert, L. & Conzemius, A. (2000, May 9). *Leading together: Developing leadership capacity in schools.* Paper presented at the Wisconsin Association for Supervision and Curriculum Development's Spring 2000 Institute, Milwaukee-Brookfield, WI.

Langford, D. P. & Cleary, B. A. (1995). *Orchestrating learning with quality.* Milwaukee: ASQ Quality Press.

McAdams, R. P. & Zinck, R. A. (1998, Fall). The power of the superintendent's leadership in shaping school district cultures: Three case studies. *ERS Spectrum 16*(3), 3.

McChesney, J. & Hertling, E. (2000, April). The path to comprehensive school reform. *Educational Leadership, 57*(7), 10–15.

Meyer, C. (1994, May–June). How the right measures help teams excel. *Harvard Business Review,* 95–103.

Murphy, C. (2000, January 19). Mendota school does a 180. *The Capital Times* (Madison, WI), B2.

Neuhauser, P. C. (1988). *Tribal warfare in organizations.* New York: Harper Business.

Newmann, F. M. & Associates. (1996). *Authentic achievement: Restructuring schools for intellectual quality.* San Francisco: Jossey-Bass.

Newmann, F. M., King, M. B., & Youngs, P. (1999, April 28). *Professional development that addresses school capacity: Lessons from urban elementary schools.* Paper presented at the annual meeting of the American Educational Research Association, New Orleans.

Newmann, F. M., Secada, W., & Wehlage, G. (1995). *A guide to authentic instruction and assessment: Vision, standards and scoring.* Madison: Wisconsin Center for Education Research.

Newmann, F. M. & Wehlage, G. (1995). *Successful school restructuring: A report to the public and educators.* Madison, WI: Wisconsin Center for Educational Research.

O'Neil, J. (2000, April). Fads and fireflies: The difficulties of sustaining change (Interview with Larry Cuban). *Educational Leadership, 57*(7), 6–9.

O'Neill, J. (2000a, February). SMART Goals, SMART Schools. *Educational Leadership, 57*(5), 46–50.

O'Neill, J. (2000b, April). Capturing an organization's oral history. *Educational Leadership, 57*(7), 63–65.

O'Neill, J. (2001, January). Three routes to results: Lie, distort, improve continuously. *The School Administrator, 58*(1), 50.

Peck, M. S. (1987). *The different drum: Community making and peace.* New York: Simon & Schuster.

Peterson, K. D. & Warren, V. (1994). Changes in school governance and principals' roles: Changing jurisdictions. New power dynamics, and conflict in restructured schools. In J. Murphy & K. S. Louis (Eds.), *Reshaping the principalship: Insights from transformational reform efforts.* Thousand Oaks, CA: Corwin Press.

Richardson, J. (2000, May). Successful schools share winning strategies (Interview with Gordon Cawelti). *Results, 6.*

Rosenholz, S. J. (1991). *Teacher's workplace: The social organization of schools.* New York: Teachers College Press.

Rossi, R. J. & Stringfield, S. D. (1995, September). What we must do for students placed at risk. *Phi Delta Kappan, 77*(1), 73–76.

Saphier, J. & D'Auria, J. (1993). *How to bring vision to school improvement.* Carlisle, MA: Research for Better Teaching.

Sarason, S. B. (1990). *The predictable failure of educational reform.* San Francisco: Jossey-Bass.

Schaffer, E. C., Nesselrodt, P. S., & Stringfield, S. C. (1997). *Impediments to reform: An analysis of destabilizing issues in ten promising programs.* Arlington, VA: Educational Research Service.

Schauble, L. (1996, November 15). Presentation at the National Institute for Science Education Interdisciplinary Teamwork Symposium, Madison, WI.

Schein, E. H. (1992). *Organizational culture and leadership.* San Francisco: Jossey-Bass.

Schein, E. H. (1997). *Organizational culture and leadership* (2nd ed.). San Francisco: Jossey-Bass.

Schmoker, M. (1996). *Results: The key to continuous school improvement.* Alexandria, VA: Association for Supervision and Curriculum Development.

Schmoker, M. (1998). *Results: The key to continuous school improvement* (2nd ed.). Alexandria, VA: Association for Supervision and Curriculum Development.

Scholtes, P. (1988). *The team handbook.* Madison, WI: Joiner Associates, Inc.

Senge, P. (1990). *The fifth discipline.* New York: Doubleday.

Senge, P. (2000). *Schools that learn.* New York: Doubleday.

Shanley, M. K. (1999, September). Students at risk: Providing the tools and support for positive change. *Curriculum Administrator, 35*(9), 38.

Sparks, D. (1999, Winter). An interview with Emily Calhoun. *Journal of Staff Development, 2*(1), 54.

Tschannen-Moran, M., Woolfolk Hoy, A., & Hoy, W. (1998). Teacher efficacy: Its meaning and measure. *Review of Educational Research 68*(2), 202–248.

Wang, M. C., Haertel, G. D., & Walberg, H. J. (1994, January). Synthesis of research: What helps students learn? *Educational Leadership, 51*(4), 74–79.

Wasley, P., Hampel, R., & Clark, R. (1997, May). The puzzle of whole-school change. *Phi Delta Kappan, 78*(9), 690–697.

Wheatley, M. J. (1992). *Leadership and the new science: Learning about organization from an orderly universe.* San Francisco: Berrett-Koehler.

White, S. D. (1999, March 9). Strategies for improving standardized test scores. [Seminar]. At the Association for Supervision and Curriculum Development Annual Conference, New Orleans.

Zemsky, R. (2000, March). The data made me do it. *Policy Perspectives 9*(2), 1–12.

Index

Note: An *f* after a page number indicates a reference to a figure.

About the Authors

The authors are the founders and managing partners of Quality Leadership by Design, LLC, where they design and implement personalized, needs-based solutions to help educational institutions, government agencies, and private sector businesses continuously improve operations. Both have professional roots in education, and together, they have devoted years of work to developing products and services schools can use to boost academic success.

Anne Conzemius, a former school psychologist, has spent many years working in quality improvement in both the public and private sectors. She has served as the Executive Assistant to the State Superintendent for the Wisconsin Department of Public Instruction, where she headed the department's strategic planning and restructuring initiative. Anne holds Master's degrees in Educational Psychology and in Industrial Relations and Human Resource Management, both from the University of Wisconsin, Madison. She is an adjunct faculty member for Cardinal Stritch University in Milwaukee.

Jan O'Neill began her career teaching elementary and middle school students and has diverse experience in early childhood education, special education, multicultural education, and the Montessori method. As an independent consultant, she pioneered the systemwide application of quality principles in municipal and state governments and in healthcare. Jan has developed and implemented numerous training and improvement efforts for public and private sector clients. She holds a Bachelor's degree in Education from Antioch College in Yellow Springs, Ohio, and a Master's degree in Public Policy and Administration from LaFollette Institute, University of Wisconsin, Madison. Jan is an adjunct faculty member for Cardinal Stritch University in Milwaukee.

You can reach Anne or Jan at QLD, Yarmouth Crossing, #188, 2935 South Fish Hatchery Road, Madison, WI 53711. E-mail: qld@qldlearning.com or visit www.QLDLearning.com.

Related ASCD Resources: Building a Professional Learning Community— School Improvement

Audiotapes

Data-Driven Decision Making by Michael Frechette, Anita Rutlin, and Mark Shibles (#200197)

Making Staff Development Part of Your School's Culture by Irv Richardson (#200134)

Seize the Data! Maximizing the Role of Data in School Improvement by Kathleen Fitzpatrick (#00169)

Staying the Course: Building a Vision of Shared Leadership for Learning by Anne Conzemius and Jan O'Neill (#201152)

Successful Teams in Diverse Schools by Vera Blake (#297185)

Online Professional Development

Go to ASCD's Home Page (http://www.ascd.org) and click on Professional Development:

ASCD Online Member Benefits: Complete text of *Educational Leadership, ASCD Curriculum Update,* and *ASCD Education Update* (password protected)

ASCD Online Professional Development Courses in *Effective Leadership, The Reflective Educator, Systems Thinking,* and *Action Research* (password protected)

ASCD Online Free Tutorials on *School Culture/Climate*

Print Products

Building Leadership Capacity in Schools by Linda Lambert (#198058)

Educators as Learners: Creating a Professional Learning Community by Michael S. Castleberry and Penelope J. Wald (#100005)

Educators Supporting Educators: A Guide to Organizing School Support Teams by Margery B. Ginsberg, Joseph F. Johnson, Jr., and Cerylle A. Moffett (#197016)

The Hero's Journey: How Educators Can Transform Schools and Improve Learning by John L. Brown and Cerylle A. Moffett (#199002)

A New Vision for Staff Development by Dennis Sparks and Stephanie Hirsh (#197018)

Professional Learning Communities at Work: Best Practices for Enhancing Student Achievement by Richard DuFour and Robert Eaker (#198188)

Results: The Key to Continuous School Improvement (2nd ed.) by Mike Schmoker (#199233)

The Results Fieldbook: Practical Strategies from Dramatically Improved Schools by Mike Schmoker (#101001)

Videotapes

Guiding School Improvement with Action Research (Books-in-Action Video) (#400215) by Richard Sagor

The Principal Series: Tape 2: Creating A Collaborative Learning Community (45 minute videotape plus Facilitator's Guide) (#498202)

The Principal Series: Tape 4: The Principal as Culture Shaper (35 minute videotape plus Facilitator's Guide) (#499238)

Schools As Communities: Teachers and Students Build a Successful School Community (two 30-minute videotapes plus Facilitator's Guide) (#499267)

For additional resources, visit us on the World Wide Web (http://www.ascd.org), send an e-mail message to member@ ascd.org, call the ASCD Service Center (1-800-933-ASCD or 703-578-9600, then press 2), send a fax to 703-575-5400, or write to Information Services, ASCD, 1703 N. Beauregard St., Alexandria, VA 22311-1714 USA.